The Story of Cork

GW00975984

The Story of Cork

BY

SEAN BEECHER

THE MERCIER PRESS,
4 BRIDGE STREET, CORK

SBN 85342 249 4

To my Mother

ACKNOWLEDGEMENTS

I would like to express my thanks to the many people who have helped me, each in their own way, to complete this book.

Mr C. J. F. McCarthy read and corrected the first draft and made numerous invaluable suggestions. Seamus Murphy also read a draft and permitted me to use his outstanding knowledge of the city and in particular its stonework. Sean Bohan and the staff of the City Library facilitated me at all times. Eilis Connally and Mrs Phil McMullen somehow succeeded in deciphiring my writing and produced typed scripts. My brother Jim helped with the research and the family tolerated all my moods. Among my friends, all of whom I cannot unfortunately mention specifically, Caoimhin O Suilleabhain agus a bhean Maire, Colm and Cris Fehilly, Dick and Ronnie Coveney, John and Anne O'Mahony and Jerry and Betty O'Suillivan have always been good to, and for, me.

Publisher and author wish to thank Capuchin Publications for permission to quote eleven verses of 'Padna' by D. L. Kelleher.

CONTENTS

CHAPTER 1

The name of the city, Cork, is derived from the Gaelic word, Corcach, meaning bog or marsh. It is located in a valley in the lower reaches of the River Lee, a district formerly known as 'Corcach Mór Mumhan' (The Great Marsh of Munster). In its virgin state, the valley, protected by steep hills rising to a height of 500 feet to the north and 300 feet to the south, consisted of twelve low-lying islands and their dividing streams. Forests of oak, elm, and ash at one time covered the slopes of the hills down to the waters edge and flourished in such profusion along the banks of the river up to the headwaters at Gougane Barra that an old chronicler could comment on squirrels coming in the valley without ever setting foot on the ground.

Finnbarr, Patron Saint of the city, ventured in along the valley from his monastery at Gougane Barra and about the year A.D. 600 founded his monastery at Cork. It was to last a thousand years. The site of this establishment is now accepted to be at Gillabbey, a rock outcrop to the south of the city centre.

The introduction of Christianity to Ireland in the fifth century brought with it the Roman script and classical learning. The new religion fused in a dynamic fashion with the old Gaelic traditions and produced a literature without parallel in the Europe of its day. In the sixth, seventh, and eighth centuries, Ireland, as yet untouched by the ravages of the Norsemen and enjoying a marvellous flowering in the arts and literature, attracted students and scholars from all over Europe, and in its turn sent back to the continent a host of Irish missionaries. As the reputation of the monastic schools spread, so the numbers attending them grew and Cork boasted of an enrolment of 400 scholars.

These early monasteries were of simple construction, enclaves surrounded by a wall or bank of stone or earth. Inside, the church was usually of stone, the various buildings for the occupants being of wattle and daub construction except where stone was readily available. They were extremely vulnerable to the attacks of the Norsemen who found them easy prey and a rich source of booty. The sacred vessels made of precious metals were particularly valuable. Initially, the Vikings limited their attacks to coastal regions, but gradually on acquiring a knowledge of the country they extended their raids inland. The unimpeded course of the River Lee brought them to Finnbarr's settlement and on a number of occasions — some historians put it at eleven — it was raided and burned. It was understandable that some of the Norsemen should settle and in the course of time they erected a fortification in Cork. Dependent on — and invincible on — water, they chose a site in the complex of islands in the centre of the valley, around what are now the North and South Main streets. It was this rather than Finnbarr's settlement at Gillabbey which was to form the nucleus of the present city. In the course of the next two centuries the Norsemen expended their energies which eventually waned in the tenth century.

The development of Cork received its next impetus with the coming of the Normans in the twelfth century. Equipped with better armour, more professional and unified in their approach and fortified with a Papal Bull, they shattered for a time the old Gaelic order. In 1185, John, Lord of Ireland and later King of England, granted the first charter to the Norman settlement of Cork. A more comprehensive charter was granted by Henry III on 2 January 1242. Granted permission to fortify the city, it appears likely that the Normans followed the general pattern of the earlier Norse fortifications while extending and strengthening them over the years. Available maps indicate the general run of the walls. Taking the North and South Main Streets as an axis, the walls ran along the near side of Grattan Street with Clarke's Bridge on the right, on to French's Quay on the east; on the west by the near side of Cornmarket Street, Grand Parade, to the South Channel of the river. Certainly the first known extant map of 1545 limits the city to this

10

area. Side streets, corresponding to the present Old Post Office Lane, Portney's, Cockpit, and Phillip's Lanes are clearly indicated.

Before the discovery of gunpowder, the city was well protected; the streams of the valley constituted natural moats and defensive positions. However, with the introduction of cannon, it was extremely vulnerable from the hills to the north and south. Shandon (from the Gaelic Sean Dun, the Old Fort) on the north, and Elizabeth Fort on the south were constructed as a permanent reminder to the citizens of their vulnerability.

The process of 'Gaelicization' or assimilation was soon in evidence. The Normans began to speak Irish; to dress in the Gaelic manner; to play Gaelic games and to intermarry with the Irish. Later, however, as the Anglo-Saxon influence began to make itself felt, the Normans themselves came under pressure and laws were enacted to inhibit their assimilation into the Gaelic way of life. The city was closed to the Irish and they were compelled to live outside the walls, on the site of the present Shandon and Blarney Streets in the north and French's Quay and Barrack Street in the south. Even to this day some of the older residents refer to Blarney Street as 'Irishtown'. The exclusion of the Irish from the city also led to the rather peculiar position whereby Norse originally, later French, later still Anglo-Saxon, and finally English were the vernaculars of the city, even though Gaelic was the medium throughout the rest of the country.

In 1690, a large tract of land, circumscribed by the present Emmet Place and the North Channel, appears for the first time on a map, together with a bowling green near the present public market on the Grand Parade. In 1720, the Mardyke, then called the Red House Walk, is shown, as is Gallows Green, off Barrack Street, then the site of public executions. This map also shows a bridge from Daunt's Square to the Grand Parade and a second bridge from Tuckey Street to Oliver Plunkett Street. The South Mall is also indicated, although the street was not covered in until 1801.

Reflecting the rather quiet period in Irish history from 1690 to the end of the eighteenth century, little development appears to have taken place in Cork, and no major land reclamations or extensions to the city took place.

Murphy's map of 1789 shows the Grand Parade, Corn-market Street, Grattan Street, Henry Street, and Patrick Street. It does appear that not all of Patrick Street had been reclaimed, as in 1830, the corporation noted the removal of a drawbridge, near the present Drawbridge Street noting that 'the timber was rotten and nearly all Patrick Street was then covered.' By the early years of the nineteenth century most of what is now the centre of the city had been reclaimed. Outside the walls, the 'Irish' quarters were acquiring a more permanent appearance. Mallow Lane (now Shandon Street), Blarney Street, and Blackpool to the north, and Barrack Street and French's Quay to the south were being extended.

The city was prospering under the comparative peace of the eighteenth century and the wealthy merchant families began to build their homes in the beautiful districts on the hills of Montenotte and Sunday's Well, while the older families, like the Coppingers, who were of Viking descent, built in Mary Street. The Sheares family built in Sheares Street (formerly Nile Street and earlier yet Mill Street) and the Emmets lived in Hammonds Marsh, now called Henry Street.

Overall, the development of the city was comparatively slow and apparently unplanned, and Graham Greene in his book *Our Man in Havana* points out that the British were inclined to allow their cities to grow, while the French and Spanish were conscious of the need for planning, with an eye for beauty as well as function. It was not until the latter half of the nineteenth century that the city began to expand to any appreciable degree, and even in the last century Sheares Villa in Glasheen Village was considered the 'country' home of that family even though it is not more than one and a half miles from the centre of the city. Other small villages which also formed a ring around the city were Bishopstown, Ballintemple, Blackrock, Ballinlough, Douglas, and Mayfield, all of which have now been integrated into the city.

The turn of the present century ushered in a new era in development, particularly as regards housing. Down through the years many of the older mansions and homes of the merchant families had fallen into decline and had been converted into flats, and later still, tenements. Areas like Harpur's Lane (now St Pauls Ave), Brown Street, the North Main Street, Bachelors Quay, Sheares Street, Peter's Street – indeed practically all the old Marsh, had degenerated into a teeming slum area. An awakening social conscience demanded their replacement, and in 1886 the first municipal housing scheme, named Madden's Buildings, was begun. In 1922 the Corporation introduced the first of its modern housing schemes – Mac Curtain Buildings. Later there was the beginning of Gurranebraher and Spangle Hill (now Farranree) Schemes. In the south, old market gardens were acquired and the extensive estate of Ballyphehane was begun. After the first World War the British Government took upon itself to provide houses for its ex-service men and constructed many homes in Fair Hill, Whitethorn (Douglas), and Haig's Gardens, Boreenmanna Road. This development was state-supported with a minimum of private investment.

Cork still suffered from a chronic shortage of adequate housing, for while the Corporation provided, to some extent at least, for the working class population, there was no adequate provision for the housing problems of the middle class. In 1948 the government belatedly introduced the Small Dwellings (Acquisition) Act, in an effort to stimulate the expansion of private, middle-class housing. Construction increased; areas immediately adjacent to the city were extensively developed, and the villages previously cut off from the city were quickly integrated. The Borough Boundary Extensions of 1954 and 1965 recognized this development by bringing these suburbs under the jurisdiction of the city administration.

Cork has for many years been considered the heavy industrial centre of the country. Originally the industries were of an agricultural nature: Food processing, woollen and other textile industries. Later there were glass, iron foundries and shipbuilding and, later still, car assembly, rubber products and an oil refinery.

A city – any city – is more than a physical development; it is the end result of an organic growth which incorporates many aspects and eventually creates a particular character. Cork has, no doubt, been influenced by the monsatic settlement, by the Norse, the Normans, the Anglo-Saxons and the Irish themselves; it has been called the most European of Irish cities – and with good reason. Its position as a sea port, and the strategic trading location with a hinterland rich in agricultural products; Catholics, Quakers, Jews, Anglicans, Presbyterians, Methodists, Baptists, Huguenots; a proliferation of industries; a strong theatrical tradition and a virile publishing history – all these have contributed to the development of what Robert Gibbings called 'the loveliest city in the world'. The people are proud, tough, sarcastic, sentimental, iconoclastic, in perpetual pursuit of self-expression, wary of intellectuals. They have travelled the world over, yet ever remember their native city. Frank O'Connor considered its mental age to be eighteen and a half, yet he himself immortalized Cork in his writings.

Unlike Dublin, Cork lacks a predominant influence. The physical appearance is as variegated as the people. 'Party-coloured like its people, red and white stands Shandon Steeple'. Yet it is this very independence which contributes to its being; as Desmond McNamara said, 'a city of tattered grace, probably the most loquacious and seductive in Western Europe'.

CHAPTER 2

Every city has a focal point. In Cork it is the 'Statue', that section of St Patrick Street where the statue of Father Mathew stands, looking towards Bridge Street and St Patrick's Hill.

Over the centuries Cork has accommodated most of the Christian denominations and many of them still hold the allegiance of citizens. It is ironic that while religious persecution was practised against the Catholics, in some degree or other, other denominations should find sanctuary in the city. The Huguenots found refuge in the city after the St Bartholomew's Day massacre in France.

The Baptist community in Cork has its church in MacCurtain Street. While it is impossible to put a definite date on their arrival in Ireland it is certain that the Baptists were in the country before Oliver Cromwell. Many more of course came in Cromwell's army. The Cork church was organized c. 1650 and the first meetings were probably held in the home of Edward Riggs of Riggsdale, Bandon. The community acquired their first church in Liberty Street on the site of the present Franciscan Friary. This church was disposed of at the end of the eighteenth century and another church built in Marlboro Street. A burial ground was also acquired in St Stephen's Street, and although it is still there, it is in a very poor condition, having been severely damaged by vandals. In 1842 the Marlboro Street church was handed over to the Plymouth Brethren but was re-opened for services in 1888. Later this church was sold to the Young Men's Christian Association and the present church in MacCurtain Street opened in 1893.

One of the most picturesque of all Cork Churches is that of the Presbyterians at the foot of Summerhill. The Presbyterians were first mentioned in Cork in 1675 and are thought to be of English extraction. It appears that they opened their first church in Dunscombes Marsh, the site of the present Oliver Plunkett Street and Princes Street, although there is mention of a church in Hanover Street at an earlier period. The church in Princes Street was subsequently rebuilt and still stands. In 1831 some of the community wished to be associated with the Church of Scotland, and in 1832 a congregation was organized and met in Tuckey Street until the church in Father Mathew Street was opened in 1841. Until this church ceased to function it was known as the 'Scots Church'. The church in Father Mathew Street in time proved too small and it was decided to erect a new one. On 28 July the church at the foot of Summerhill was opened. It is a beautiful building, incorporating local, Portland and Bath stone, and it was designed by the architect Tarring. An unusual feature is that the spire is slightly curved, an error made by a stonemason.

The Lower Road, undistinguished by the high houses flanking one side and the greyness of the Harbour Board Yard, ends abruptly at 'The Ferry Boat Inn'. Suddenly one finds oneself in the open space of Tivoli on the north bank of the Lee. Years ago a ferry operated a regular service across the river, taking the patrons to and from the hurling games in the Athletic Grounds, but the insurance companies demanded too high a premium and the family business closed down. Across the river which is now widening before it debouches into the broad expanse of Lough Mahon, the quaint timber structures of the Lee Rowing and Shandon Boat Clubs are anachronistic against the backdrop of the Marina Industrial Estate. Not so long ago this stretch of the river was one of the most famous rowing courses where European Clubs came to contest the 'Leander Cup'. Now, despite much better travel facilities, foreign crews are a rarity. A green grassy bank stretches away in a long slow curve; the tall elm trees are parallel and on the top of a grassy knoll, close by the bandstand, an old cannon lies on its side — a relic of the Crimean War.

Much of the slob land on the north bank of the river has already been reclaimed, much more is in the course of reclamation and, within the next few years, the Cork Harbour

Board will construct an Industrial estate and despoil the beautiful natural reaches of the river. Already householders in Blackrock, on the far side of the river, have sold their property, fearful that the new development, by reducing the scenic amenities of the area, will devalue their property.

At the beginning of the nineteenth century, Woodhill House was the home of a Quaker family (Cooper-Penrose) who were friends of John Philpott Curran, the most brilliant advocate of his day. Due to its numerous art treasures, Woodhill House was known as 'The Irish Vatican'. All that remains is a ruined shell and it is known as the 'Haunted House'.

In 1803, Curran, on learning of his daughter Sarah's secret engagement to the revolutionary Robert Emmet and disapproving of his politics, sent her to live at Woodhill House. Sarah Curran broke her engagement to Emmet and he returned to Dublin and led his insurrection which lasted but three hours. Emmet was captured and tried and, of course, found guilty of treason and executed. At his trial, before the infamous hanging judge, Norberry, he made one of the most brilliant orations in Irish history and concluded: 'Let no man write mine epitaph, for as no man who knows my motives dares now vindicate them; let not ignorance nor prejudice disperse them; let them rest in obscurity and peace until other times and other men can do justice to my character. Then, and not till then, let mine epitaph be written.' In the course of his speech, Emmet, denying that the insurrection was merely an extension of the French Revolution and indeed an attempt to organize a rebellion which would facilitate the French in their wars against the English, insisted that Irish Republicanism was indigenous and that Irish Republicanism would resist imperialism, be it French or English or that of any other country: 'Were the French to come as invaders or enemies, uninvited by the wishes of the people, I should oppose them to the utmost of my strength. Yes, my countrymen, I should advise you to meet them upon the beach with a sword in one hand and a torch in the other. I would meet them with all the destructive fury of war. I would animate my countrymen to immolate them in their

17

boats, before they had contaminated the soil of my country. If they succeeded in landing, and if forced to retire before superior discipline, I would dispute every inch of the ground, burn every blade of grass, and the last entrenchment of liberty should be my grave.'

This portion of the speech shows an uncanny similarity to that delivered by Winston Churchill during the last war. The Irishman Brendan Bracken was Churchill's speechwriter at the time and must have been familiar with Emmet's great oration. It does seem likely that Bracken culled this portion from Emmet, paraphrased it and presented it to Churchill for delivery. One wonders if Churchill appreciated the irony of the situation.

Certainly the Cork Corporation were unmoved by Emmet's oratory, in fact they conferred the Freedom of the City on the prosecuting attorney, O'Grady.

Tivoli House, reputedly the sometime home of Walter Raleigh, is situated off Lovers' Walk (formerly the Lepers' Road). Raleigh is reputed to have smoked the first pipefull of tobacco in the 'Old World' in this house but this has been contested by Youghal. An illustration in the *Graphic* of a century ago indicates that a reputed set of Raleigh's pipes were then in existence.

Raleigh was a pirate in the days of the 'virgin' Queen Elizabeth I, known in Irish as Beiti na Muice, Betty of the Pig. Raised to the knighthood for his success in hi-jacking Spanish galleons on the high seas, he was granted an extensive estate of 12,000 acres which he is said to have increased to 42,000 acres in the counties of Cork and Waterford. This was part of the Munster Plantation following the Desmond confiscation when English 'undertakers', largely Court hangers on, were granted Munster lands. Later the granting of substantial tracts of Irish land was an expedient much favoured by the British Crown to pay off creditors and by the Kings to pay off their mistresses. It is interesting that the descendants of these settlers consider themselves – and are considered – the 'aristocrats' of Ireland. Even to this day, despite the work of Michael Davitt, much property is still in the hands of planters and people of non-Irish descent whose only justification for possession is the questionable legality of these confiscations. Blarney Castle, an internationally known landmark and for many people synonymous with Ireland, is but one example. It enjoys a very substantial income from tourism and should be taken over by the State, declared a national Monument and the revenue used for the upkeep of our ancient monuments. The Desmond Attainter Act by which thousands of acres became Crown property has never been repealed. The government has in the past fifty years repealed many pre-1800 acts but it has said that the repeal of the Desmond Confiscation Act 'could present difficulties'.

Lover's Walk joins Montenotte, called in Irish, Cnoc An Atinn, the Hill of the Furze. Montenotte is in the townland of Ballinabocht, the Town of the Poor, yet it has always been the residence of the wealthy merchants of Cork. During the Penal Days head leases there forbade anyone, other than a Protestant, to build a house; a Papist could build a cabin. Looking down on the river from here the Customs House indicates the eastern extremity of the main island of the city.

Many of the old mansions of Montenotte have not survived as family residences. The excessive cost of labour, (excessive in relation to the pre trade-union days when scandalous wages and conditions obtained) and the high cost of maintenance and the demands of 'mod-cons', have contributed to their being remodelled into hotels, guest houses and flats.

The concial shaped hut at St Lukes Cross is one of the few remaining toll-houses. For centuries these toll-houses ringed the city, located at all main entrances. The laws required that farmers, bringing livestock into the city should pay a fee. The amount of the fee varied over the years, but in the early days of the last century it was one penny per head of cattle and a halfpenny per head on sheep and pigs. In many European countries the collection of urban tolls was a privilege of religious orders, but in Ireland it was a municipal privilege. While most of these toll-houses have actually disappeared, there are one or two remaining.

CHAPTER 3

Dillon's Cross is named in memory of the patriot Brian Dillon. The district is dominated by the presence of the military barracks, now named Collin's Barracks in memory of Michael Collins. For a century it was the seat of British Imperialism in the south of the country, dominating and influencing the people. It was here that the first soccer team in the city was founded – Barrackton. Initially the team consisted entirely of British soldiers but later many of the locals participated. Their great rivals were St Vincents, now members of the Gaelic Athletic Association, and Republican in their sympathies. During one of their more strenuous encounters, with the scores level, a Barrackton forward broke through the Vincents' defence. With only the goalkeeper to beat he paused to take aim, whereupon a Vincentian Republican supporter, fearful of the result, drew a revolver and shot the ball!

In a glorious compliment, Yeats once said that Frank O'Connor did for Irish literature what Checkov did for Russia. O'Connor lived in a small house in Harrington's Square just short of Dillon's Cross. Many of his short stories are set in this locality, and, indeed, some of them reflect the influence of the military presence. O'Connor, while still attending St Patrick's National School, came under the influence of Daniel Corkery. In a short time he was producing and proving himself to be one of the finest exponents of short-story writing in the world. To this medium he added plays, novels, and criticism. In his later period he devoted his time to biography, autobiography and – probably his most brilliant and most enduring success of all – the translation of the old Gaelic poetry. O'Connor was such a prolific writer and successful in so many ways that it is difficult to asses his real value, to anticipate the place he will hold in the world's literature. Some of his short stories are real gems but he did stray from the influence of Corkery and came under the influence of *The New Yorker,* a fact which may have lessened his expression and affected his reputation. But his translations of old Gaelic poetry are so superb that it may be that his reputation will be paramount in this field.

In 1967 Goulding's Glen, an extensive depression once used by the army as a training ground, was handed over by the owners, Goulding's Fertilisers, to the Corporation. It is to be developed by the local authority as a playground and amenity.

Audley Terrace at the top of Patrick's Hill affords one of the most dramatic and panoramic views of the city. It is spread out from the docks in the east to the burgeoning valley of the Lee to the west. There are the churches of Shandon, St Marys, St Peter and Paul's, St Francis's, St Finbarrs, Farrenree, Gurranebraher, Dennehy's Cross, St Vincent's; there are the Opera House, Murphy's Brewery, Blackpool Valley, and, on the brow of the hills to the north, the extensive housing schemes of Farranree and Gurranebraher, and in the distance to the west the Bishopstown housing are seen. Alongside Audley Terrace there is Rathmore Place which together with Hibernian Buildings was the first major housing project, built privately in the city. Two hundred houses were built at a cost of £24,000.

Like a ski-jump, Patricks Hill drops away from Audley Terrace to the centre of the city. It is a rather French-style boulevard, the footpaths terraced to facilitate pedestrians, lined by trees and the homes and consulting rooms of the city's doctors. For many years the local cycling association sponsored an annual hill climb. From a standing start at the foot it was a speed test to the summit. Another group of cyclists − now fast disappearing and with them a good deal of local colour − were the errand or messengers boys. They too were interested in testing themselves against Patrick's Hill but in a less arduous if at the same time much more dangerous manner than the cyclists. On their specially constructed bicycles, sturdy and tough with the front wheel smaller than the rear one, and a large basket suspended over it, they loved to come careering down the hill and

21

along Patrick's Street in free-wheel, a competition to ascertain who could travel the greatest distance without propulsion. More often than not, they carried a passenger sitting in the basket and often a second on the cross-bar. When the Garda Siochana at point duty at the foot of the hill saw them approaching he had little option but to let discretion be the better part of valour, halt all traffic *en route* and allow the messenger boys right of way! The hill itself is so steep that when it was being opened to permit access to Audley Terrace it had to be vaulted. The entrance to these vaults is from Coburg Street.

Patrick's Street is only a stone's throw from that ancient part of Cork, Blackpool. The finest example of the Cork accent is to be found in Blackpool. Similar in some respects to the Welsh, and often confused with it in its rhythmic up-and-down cadences, it is quite different to any other Irish accents. There is a pronounced flattening of the 'a' vowel and the 'th' sounds are always pronounced 'd', so that we find 'dis, dat, dese, and dose' in widespread use throughout the city. Blackpool played a significant part in the economic recovery of the city in the nineteenth century. In the last century there were many tanneries in the city and most of them were located in Blackpool; there were the tanneries of Murphy's, Lyons, Hegarty's, The Glen Tannery and Boot Manufactury (Ryans), and most successful of all, Dunn Brothers. The famine of the 1840s and the importation of cheap ready made boots heralded the end of this industry. The manufacture of textiles was also associated with the district, particularly after the Act of Union, and there was intensive manufacture of broadcloth, blankets, flannels, hosiery, checks, threads, braid, and rope. The district retains its tradition with the operation of Sunbeam Wolsey in the present day.

Gouldings Fertilisers were established in Blackpool in 1854 and much of the raw material: sulphur from Spain, Phosphate from Florida, and bones from India was imported. The traditions of brewing and distilling are centuries old. Hewitt's distillery, until it amalgamated with the Cork Distilleries company, was in the Watercourse Road. Murphy's Brewery was established in 1854. The brewery buildings in the Watercourse Road are situated on the site of an old Foundling Hospital: Over the years, when the original function of the buildings had been forgotten, the rumour had it that all the unwanted illegitimate babies were disposed of by depositing them in Murphy's Brewery.

Blackpool Church is a gift to the city from the late William Dwyer, and the building was designed by Seamus Murphy, whose studios are also in the Watercourse Road.

Directly across from the Church, on the Watercourse Road is the house in which Tomas MacCurtain, Lord Mayor of Cork, was murdered by British forces in 1920. Blackpool is also the parish of that most dedicated and successful of hurling teams, Glen Rovers.

Most cities the world over are associated with particular buildings or monuments and Cork is no exception. Shandon Steeple has become synonymous with the city. Towering over a complex of narrow laneways and small factories, it is situated in one of the most interesting areas in the city. The name Shandon is derived from the Gaelic, Sean Dun, meaning 'the old fort', and it was situated on the site of the present margarine factory, across the road. Shandon was originally a stronghold of the Norman family, Barry, and the Lord President of Munster held court here. In 1588, all those associated with the Desmond Rebellion were tried here, largely *in absentia,* and their lands attainted. After this rebellion — which effectively destroyed the power of the old Norman families — the way was open for the Plantation of Munster and the consolidation of the Anglo-Saxon conquest. Shandon is a peculiar, pepperpot construction, erected in 1770, the south and west sides facing the prevailing winds built in red sandstone, the north east in limestone. Rumour has it that two contractors, one owning a sandstone quarry, the other a limestone quarry, agreed to share the contract and accordingly the supply of material. The weathervane is in the shape of a goldfish and motivated Donal Giltinan, to title a play *Goldfish in the Sun.* The clock, built and installed by the jewellers, Mangans of Patrick Street, has four faces, none of which show the same time and earned for Shandon the nickname 'The Four-faced Liar'. There is a carillion of eight bells, made at the foundry of Abel Rudd of Gloucester, which may be played by local or tourist alike. Probably the song most associated with the city is 'The Bells of Shandon'. It was written by a Catholic priest, Father Mahony who wrote under a pen-name 'Father Prout'. Father Mahony was a somewhat unusual clergyman. He retired from the priesthood, went to London, where he was a most successful journalist, travelled extensively on the continent, was a brilliant linguist and eventually was received back into the church. He was buried in the Protestant graveyard in Shandon.

Skiddy's Home, L-shaped, steep-roofed, colonnaded, is the oldest inhabited building in the city. At one time it was a complex of three charitable institutions but one of these 'The Green Coat School' was razed. In 1967 an attempt was made to demolish Skiddy's Home and build a nurses home on the site but the efforts of the local preservation committee were successful and a preservation order was granted. Three limestones plaques in the walls tell the story of Skiddy's.

> This part of the Almshouse belongs to the foundation of Mr Clement Skiddy, alias Scudamore, who about the year of Our Lord MDCXX(1620) settled a perpetual amount of £24 paid by the vintners of London for the benefit of twelve aged widows of this city.
> 'The end of the Commandment is Charity.'

Another plaque reads:

> In this part of the building are lodged 7 old Protestant soldiers for whose support and apprenticing Poor Protestant children, Capt. Roger Bretridge gave an estate of £63 per annum for ever. A.D. MDCLXXX (1690)
> 'The Righteous shall be held in everlasting rememberance.' Psalm 112.

The recipients of Bretridges were housed in the ground floor portion of the almshouse. Outside the gate of 'The Green Coat School' were two lead statues, representative of the school and familiarly known as 'Bob and Joan'. The statues were four feet high and a local jingle had it

'Mary Budd and William Heavey
Made of lead and very heavy.'

When the building was being demolished, the authorities, fearing that the statues would be damaged, lost or stolen had them removed to Shandon Steeple where they are now lodged, cemented into the floor of the bell-tower. 'Bob and Joan' were to add a new phrase to the patois of the north side of the city as courting couples, desirous of privacy, were accustomed to dally in the secluded laneway flanking Skiddy's and so 'Bob and Joan' took on a different meaning.

The Butter Exchange Market is probably one of the most interesting of commercial buildings in the city. It is now a hat factory and gives little indication of its former stature when in the last century it was the centre of the world's butter trade. The limestone walls are plastered, some of the arches have been sealed, all these changes taking from its appearance. The Cork Butter Market was originally instituted by the local merchants on a voluntary basis. The regulations were stringently enforced and a breach was severely punished – the identity of the culprit and details of his chicanery were published in the local newspapers. At a later date when the market was granted legal authority: defaulters were convicted in the courts of law. While the quality of Cork butter may not necessarily have been superior to other Irish or foreign butters, the reputation of Cork butter was based on the uniform standards maintained in the classification and grading. This system of grading was rigidly enforced and conducted in strictest secrecy. All samples were numbered and the identity of the merchants was kept secret from the inspectors who themselves earned a high salary – in 1815 it was £420 p.a. – a substantial amount in those days. The inspectors were in turn subject to checking and a penalty was imposed for poor judgement or conspiracy. There were several grades – the lowest called for some forgotten reason 'a bishop'. The butter was supplied by the farmers from as far west as Dingle in County Kerry and it was quite usual for women to walk in from Macroom, a distance of twenty-five miles. The merchants who formed the Cork Butter Exchange normally acted as agents for the farmers, supplied the firkins, gave credit, and took care of the various clerical arrangements. The butter was usually packed in firkins or kegs weighing about eighty pounds and was brought in to market on horseback, the men walking non-stop throughout the day and night. To facilitate the farmers on their irregular arrival, the market remained open twenty-four hours a day.

From Cork Harbour the butter was shipped to every corner of the world. In addition to the consistency in grading, Cork butter appears to have had an advantage over its competitors in that it could withstand the long sea voyages much better and arrive still in an edible condition. Before America achieved self-suffiency, Cork had a virtual monopoly of its trade, and when this trade was exhausted the butter was shipped to India, Australia, New Zealand, and the Far East. Stanley is said to have found a Cork Butter firkin in Darkest Africa!

Over the years the market suffered many fluctuations in fortune. It was always at the mercy of the British vested interests and sanctions were regularly imposed to inhibit its development and function. At the time when a more benevolent or less malicious, administration, or the vagaries of international commerce warranted, the sanctions would be removed and the market permitted to recover once more. The market was in decline in the latter half of the nineteenth century; many of its principal markets achieved suffiency; the competition from Denmark and Holland was increasing. It ceased to function in the early part of this century.

Coopering, the manufacture and maintenance of the firkins, kegs, and barrels, was an essential subsidiary to the Butter Market. At one time there were 800 coopers in the city – the census of 1871 records 564 coopers. In the immediate vicinity of the market, the parish of St Mary's, there were 45 coopers. Not all of the coopers were working in the Butter Market, many of them being engaged in the brewing industry. Indeed the making of porter barrels demanded a higher degree of skill. It was called 'wet coopering' and the butter trade was called 'dry coopering'. The wages of a cooper in the parish of St Mary's in 1834 was 3/6 per day and it compared more than favourably with similar rates of pay in both Ireland and England.

Coopering is now a dead trade in Cork; the loss of the foreign markets, the introduction of the butter box which made the skill redundant, and the introduction of the 'iron lung' or aluminium barrel to the brewing trade contributed to its demise. Fortunately all the tools associated with the trade have been preserved and a selection are on display in the city museum in Fitzgerald's Park.

Here too in this old part of Cork is the headquarters of the Butter Exchange National Band which for generations was associated with the Market but fortunately has survived it. The band is not now up to the high standards of former times, many of its great characters, Jack Dineen on tuba and 'Da Billy' lead side drummer, spick and span and his moustache waxed to the envy of Hercule Poirot, have gone to their rest. 'The Loft', home of the Cork Shakespearian Company, founded by that archetypal Corkman Father Christy Flynn, and Mecca of all aspiring actors, is only around the corner from the Butter Market.

CHAPTER 4

St Mary's, generally known as the North Chapel, is the seat of the Catholic Bishop of the diocese and is the fourth church to stand since the Reformation. The first was erected in 1635, probably in Coppingers Lane. It was followed by another in Old Chapel Lane in 1700 and the third was built on the present site in 1730. In 1808 the present church was dedicated by Bishop Moylan 'with a solemnity unequalled in these islands'. It is in the pointed Gothic style and the nave was then 109 feet long and 62 feet wide. In 1820 the building was damaged by fire and it was subsequently renovated by George Pain. The church has not been completed in accordance with the original designs but the tower was added in 1862-7 and a peal of nine bells, 'cast by J. Murphy, Founder, Dublin', was later included in the tower. The baptismal records extend as far back as 1748 and are invaluable to local historians.

Some notable men have ministered in this parish. There was the Bishop John Butler, twelfth Lord Dunboyne, who was consecrated in 1763. In 1786, then over seventy years of age, he succeeded to the title and estates. He sought approval from Rome to marry and, being refused, he resigned his See and conformed to the Protestant church in Clonmel in 1787. In 1800 he was received back into the church and died the same year. In his will, which was contested but settled amicably, he bequeathed £1,000 p.a. to found the Dunboyne Establishment in Maynooth.

Bishop John Murphy who reigned from 1815 to 1845 was a great patron of Gaelic culture. He commissioned Michael O Longain to assemble one of the finest collections of old Irish manuscripts and then offered them to the diocese on the condition that a library would be established for them. Unfortunately this offer was not accepted, and while some of these invaluable documents are now in Maynooth the majority have been sold recently and are now scattered.

During the recent renovations to the church when an extra twenty-five feet was added to the sanctuary at a cost of £250,000 and the despoilation of its appearance many of the tablets and statues were damaged. Among them the statue of Dr Murphy, Hogan's last work, executed, it is thought, in gratitude for his efforts, in conjunction with Sharman Crawford, for financing Hogan's studies in Rome. Another tablet now restored was in memory of Father John England, late Bishop of Charlestown, U.S.A., who played such an important part in the Catholic Emancipation debates of the 1820s.

Father Christy Flynn, who founded the Cork Shakespearian Company, was a curate here for many years. He was a great advocate of the Gaelic language and music, learning his Irish from a native speaker Mrs O'Sullivan who lived in the old and now razed Corbett's Lane. Father Christy was well known for his skill in curing speech impediments. Cynics say that the put such a fear of God in the sufferers that they forgot their impediments and spoke normally. Nor was he above taking off his coat and chastising a husband who was ill-treating a wife. His knowledge of Shakespearian drama was authorative and many of the most renowned actors of the day, the McMasters, and MacLiammoirs whenever they played in Cork, regularly visited the 'loft'. Father O'Flynn, it appears, was inclined to take minor liberties with Shakespeare's text, changing words which he thought were too 'strong'. On one occasion when he had had the actor substitute 'harlot' for 'whore' a visiting actor chided him 'Father, why not whore, why not whore, Father?'

On another occasion the Company put on six Shakesperian plays in one week – a truly fantastic achievement for an amateur group. It was inevitable that trouble should arise in the filling of bitparts and on the night when Macbeth was being performed the person who was to play the messenger to bring the news of Birnam Wood failed to arrive. They went out into the streets, literally, to find an actor and eventually persuaded or coerced a passer-by to help. This gentleman was very sceptical, 'Me play in the Opera House? Is it codding me you are?' Eventually, after much coaxing, threatening, and some money having passed, he permitted himself to have a cloak put around his shoulders, a sword put in his hand and to be coached to say his line, 'My Lord, Birnam Wood hath moved to Dunsinane'. At the time of his entry he was pushed on to the stage and, falling on his knees, he declaimed his lines. The king, seeing the fulfillment of the prophecy, began to rant and rave and succeeded in intimidating the poor actor, who fearful for his life shouted, 'Sir 'twasn't my fault at all, 'twas the fellows out there told me what to say!'

St Mary's Road runs past the convent of St Vincent's, a school dedicated to the education of the girls of the north side of the city. For many years the nuns performed a very useful function in the social life of the young boys and girls of the parish, sponsoring weekly dances in what became known as the 'Oratory'. In time the 'Oratory' became an institution creating a style of dancing all its own and its devotee's could be recognized in any dance hall in the city by their technique. The dances were strictly supervised by a member of the order who in her own right became an institution also. She remainded on duty for a considerable time ensuring that the dancers remained the statutory six inches apart. In the ladies cloakroom a notice proclaimed 'No low necklines of sleeveless cardigans permitted' but when the good nun had made her final tour of inspection there was generally a rush to the cloakroom and the girls divested themselves of their protective garments. The rosary was also said in the course of the night.

Close by St Vincent's is the Monastery of Our Lady's Mount, the school of the Christian Brothers, known nationally as the 'North Mon'. The Order of the Christian Brothers was founded in 1811 in Waterford by Edmund Ignatius Rice to provide education for the poor. For over a century and a half they gave a free – or as free as makes no difference – education to the people of Ireland. The Christian Brothers are the largest teaching order in the country and with its complex of primary and secondary and technical schools they contribute an enormous share to education,

30

and under the umbrella of the Hierarchy they constitute the most effective educational lobby in the country. It was, and indeed still is a truism to say that the civil service is run by Corkmen and many of these civil servants are products of the schools of the Christian Brothers and in particular the 'North Mon'. The charge is often made that the Brothers sacrificed a liberal education for the sake of success at examinations, that too much emphasis was put on cramming and that, at times, the welfare of the less gifted was sacrificed for the benefit of the cleverer pupil. Whether of not the charge can be substantiated it is necessary to appreciate the social conditions which motivated the brothers and contributed to this situation. The purpose of the order was to provide an education for the poor. But if man does not exist on bread alone, neither does he exist without it. They were faced with a two-fold problem: providing an education and at the same time an education which would enable their pupils to better themselves. The business community was dominated by nepotism and social standing to such an extent that the phrase 'It isn't what you know, it's who you know' was accepted as gospel. The only alternative was the government services at least the basic grades were competitive and all entrants enjoyed an equal opportunity. The brothers conformed and achieved great success in this field. An important criticism which may be levelled at the Order is that they appear to have made little effort to reform the system of education although Pearse himself had published his most famous pamphlet *The Murder Machine* back in the second decade of the century.

The Catholic Bishop lives in a modest palace in Redemption Road, near to the Diocesan seminary of St Finnbarr's, at the periphery of one of the largest Corporation housing areas in the city. The Corporation commenced their building programme in the 1930s in an effort to rid the city centre of its worst slums. These housing schemes, though admirable when compared to the slums which they replaced, show a severe lack of planning awareness and foresight. The lay-out particularly of the earlier schemes is of a very rudimentary nature: long straight streets, unbroken by any attempt at variation, the houses all identical, of a dull uniform grey. And most of the earlier schemes are not equipped with bathrooms, nor indeed have the authorities made any effort to improve the situation. However, the corporation have made efforts to remedy the position and while still inhibited by lack of finance and an unwillingness to experiment with design many of the more recent schemes are superior in lay-out to the private housing schemes in the city.

The concentration of Corporation housing schemes in particular areas of the city has created a problem which should have been anticipated. It has contributed to the stratification and segregation of the various social groups and has not been conducive to the evolution of a community spirit. Some of these corporation areas live under a social cloud and many employers discriminate against the residents on no other grounds than that of residence. It is not unusual for employers to deny positions in their firms to talented and qualified applicants merely because they reside in public housing estates.

The newly constructed church of 'The Resurrection' in Farranree is one of the most successful of the city's new churches. It was designed originally for Dublin, having been placed first in a competition organized by the Institute of Architects, under the patronage of the Archbishop John Charles McQuaid. However the Archbishop refused to accept the design and eventually the Architects' Association prevailed upon the Bishop of Cork to accept the design. It is an interesting building, with low side walls and a steep slated roof surmounted by a rather Germanic looking tower. Seen from certain parts of the city, silhouetted in the twilight it resembles a great space rocket ready to blast off and is known locally as 'Connie's Rocket'.

The corporation housing schemes stretch all along the hills to the north of the city as far west as the old Blarney Road, incorporating older districts like Fair Hill, and in the process replacing Corbetts, Burn, and Syves lanes. As recently as 1955 all this was pasture land, the lower Cathedral Road area at one time being an open air cattle market and the memory is still retained in Cattle Market Street and Cattle Market Ave. The Parochial Hall in Churchfield is an outstanding example of the spirit of co-operative and voluntary effort which has played a conspicuous if largely unknown part in the life of the city. Many achievements in the city, – the eradication of diphteria, the construction of hospitals, and recently the foundation of the Cork Polio and General After Care association were purely voluntary efforts by the citizens. The Parochial Hall, the biggest auditorium in the city, was constructed entirely by the local people, the tradesmen and others contributing their expertise and time and labour to this effort.

The Church of the Ascension in Churchfield, one of the 'Rosary' of churches which were constructed in the new housing areas is a rather plain unadorned edifice and dominates the north-west skyline of the city. The illuminated cross on its tower acts as a beacon for the airport, and it is unfortunate that an opportunity was lost to provide the city with a simply fantastic viewing balcony when the tower was being constructed. The church on the skyline of the city is situated at an old altitude of 500 feet and affords the most dramatic and panoramic view of the city. Unfortunately, the tower is accessible only by ladder, a fact which precludes visitors from gaining access. Again the view from the windows is obscured by fixed timber shutters. To the north, to east and west and down to the city centre, the red, tiled roofs of the council houses stretch away and indicate why this part of Cork is called 'The Red City'.

Baker's Lane marks the north-west boundary of the city and the view particularly that of St Finnbarr's Cathedral is really magnificent. Blarney Street, even yet called 'Irishtown' by some of its older inhabitants, is one of the areas where the native Irish settled when excluded from the city itself. Many of the houses are small terrace-types, their windows even smaller, a relic of the times when the rent was calculated on the size of the windows. This was called 'window tax'. This street was formerly the principal road to Blarney and Kerry and in fact is still referred to as the old Kerry Road. Across the road from The Good Shepherds'

33

Convent is a plaque commemorating the memory of Spriggs, a member of the I.R.A. who was taken from his home and murdered by British Forces. He was nineteen years of age. Ballycannon is not far further out the road. This was the scene of an infamous ambush when the British forces captured and then mutilated a group of Republican soldiers. It is somewhat ironic that so many of our elder statesmen belittle the youth of today, doubting their idealism and efforts. Have they forgotten that they themselves were the youth of their generation, that Spriggs was a 'boy' of nineteen when he lost his life, that Kevin Barry was eighteen years of age, that General Tom Barry was a mere twenty-two years old when he commanded the Third West Cork Brigade?

The road continues due west past Clogheen Church and the view to the south and west, overlooking the Lee Valley, and the mountains of West Cork is extensive and beautiful. About a mile past Clogheen Church, at the old forge, a road runs down to the Jewish and Catholic cemeteries of Curraghpippane. In the catholic cemetery, Jerome Collins lies buried. His grave is marked by a Celtic Cross which faces north-south, the other tombstones are faced in the traditional east-west fashion. Collins lived in the North Main Street and was Clerk of Works on the construction of the former North Gate Bridge. He was a member of the Fenians and the Irish Republican Brotherhood, that secret and shadowy organization which toiled in apparent obscurity until it organized the Rebellion of 1916. After the abortive rebellion of 1867 Collins emigrated to America and specialized in the little appreciated science of meteorology. He organized and participated in an expedition to the North Pole but died in Siberia where he was buried. At a later date an expedition was dispatched to recover his body and it was interred in New York. Later still it was felt that Collins should be laid to rest in his native city and the body was once more exhumed and returned to Cork and finally laid to rest in this graveyard. The funeral, from Siberia to New York to Cork is considered to have been the longest in history. Conversely, when the caretaker died many years ago, he was buried outside his own back window – the shortest funeral, certainly in Cork.

Continuing past the graveyard on this beautiful tree-lined roadway one arrives on the Lee Road, running parallel with the river and on a lower level than the Blarney Road. Across the valley the County Hall, Ireland's tallest building, dominates the valley. There is a right-of-way along both banks of the river and most of the land on the south bank is a gift to the citizens from an anonymous donor. The Irish Industrial and Agricultural Exhibition was held here and the first electric railway was demonstrated at the exhibition.

The Lee Road affords a beautiful view of the valley and along its length there is a series of fifteen tablets depicting the fifteen mysteries of the rosary. On 15 August, the Feast of the Assumption, each year, the Catholic Bishop leads a procession to the grotto where Benediction is celebrated. The plaques are so placed that a person, at normal walking pace, may recite a decade of the rosary between them.

The frontage of Our Lady's Hospital is said to be the longest in the country although it was originally designed as three separate buildings, the buildings being incorporated as one unit at a much later date.

The city water-works across the road from the hospital is situated at the concourse of the north and south channels of the river. Davis (though still known locally as Wellington) Bridge is the first of the five bridges which span the north channel. Wellington, the 'Iron Duke' was not, it appears, appreciative of his Irish birth and on one occasion when taxed with this unpalatable fact, commented, 'if one is born in a stable it does not necessarily mean one is a horse.'

Thomas Davis, born in Mallow in 1813 was with Gavan Duffy, founder of the newspaper *The Nation*. He was a graduate of Trinity College and a leader on the Young Ireland Movement in the 1840s. He wrote extensively for *The Nation,* particularly ballads and poems, many of which are still popular. His influence of the independence movement was enormous, despite his early death at thirty-two years of age, in 1845 and prior to the Young Ireland insurrection.

The suburb of Shanakiel (from the Gaelic, Sionnach Coill, the wood of the foxes) on the north bank of the north channel is one of the most beautiful and select areas of the city. It was originally developed as a residential district of the merchant families of Cork. Sunday's Well, another of these residential areas, was formerly known as Stable Lane. It took this name from the number of stables fronting into the roadway. A holy well was situated on this site but in the course of road-widening it was sealed off. An old tradition has it that on Easter Sunday morning at daybreak, the sun, celebrating the birth of the Risen Christ, danced for joy on Sunday's Well.

The white suspension bridge spanning the river from Sunday's Well to the Mardyke was a gift to the city from the Daly family. The Daly Bridge, erected in 1927 to replace a ferry service, is generally known as the 'Shaky Bridge' and has been the scene of many a young lady's feigned discomfort, the young boys swinging from the cables causing it to sway and evoke cries of simulated terror from the girls.

On the south bank of the north channel is the famed Mardyke, renowned in song and story but in particular by the song, Cork's own anthem, 'The Banks of my own Lovely Lee'.

How oft do my thoughts in their fancy take flight,
To the home of my childhood away
To the days when each patriots vision seem bright
Ere I dreamed that these joys could decay.
When my heart was as light as the wild winds that blow
Down the Mardyke, through each elm tree
Where I sported and played, neath the green leafy shade
On the Banks of my own lovely Lee.

The Mardyke was originally known as the Red House Walk and took this name from a tea-house or tea-garden in the vicinity. It was formed in 1720 by Edward Webber, a city official. It was a beautiful avenue, measuring a mile, flanked by the famous elm trees and by a stream running along its length. At the eastern city end, a triple gateway, known as 'Hell, Heaven and Purgatory' all but sealed it from vehicular traffic. Within the past twenty years the city authorities removed the gateway and opened up the Mardyke to traffic. At the same time the famous trees became infected by the 'Dutch Elm' disease and this necessitated their removal. The Mardyke is not now even a pale reflection of its former beauty. The Fitzgerald Municipal Park flanks the city side of the Mardyke. In addition to a childrens' playground it contains a very nice garden and a building in which is located the Cork Public Museum. There is also a permanent exhibition of sculpture in the grounds.

CHAPTER 5

One of the most pleasant distractions of life in Cork is the presence of the many characters who have contributed to the entertainment of the citizens over the years. They have come in all the different shapes and sizes, from the gently ubiquitous to the boisterously exhibitionist. Some consciously, others quite innocently, have projected their image before public attention and earned for themselves the much envied soubriquet of a 'character'.

John W. Reidy entered the public scene in the 1950s. Rumours proliferated as to his recent history and financial sources but the purchase of two dance halls, one in the city the other in the village of Carrigaline along with the acquisition of a hotel set all doubts at rest. The most accepted story, and one which appealed to the people, had it that John W. had spent the war years on the German occupied Channel Islands, availing of the benefits conferred by his Irish passport of neutrality and fortified by a native cunning, played off the British against the Germans and in the process accumulated a massive fortune. As neither the British nor the Germans would oblige popular curiosity and set the record straight John W., displaying an instinctive appreciation of human nature declined to elaborate and like the illusionist, titillated without satisfying. Soon he was a near-legendary figure, his *bonhomie* and generosity proverbial: tall and corpulent striding the city streets, exhibitionist and extrovert. But success in business could never satisfy the egotist in him and his thoughts turned to politics. He set his sights on the Municipality, possibly as a forerunner to the Dail itself. Like a true man of the people, John W. campaigned under the slogan 'The needy need Reidy, and Reidy needs your votes!'

His public meetings were an entertainment in themselves. Preceded by the massed bands of the city, one of them an up-and-coming group now known nationally as The Dixie-landers, John W. paraded his cavalcades through the streets to his destination in Patrick's Street. He insisted that only the independent candidate could afford to speak for the people, that he alone was uncommitted, that his alone would be the voice of independence and integrity, that he would protect their interests.

'They'll try to shut me up, but I won't shut up. They can throw me into the river but I won't drown. I'm fat, I'll float.'

In a city accustomed to political idiosyncrasies he was irresistible. John W. was elected an Alderman of Cork.

There is another familiar figure in the city, fortunately still with us. He is to be seen almost every day, a small figure shuffling through the streets or sitting reading in the reference room of the library. He is a frequent visitor to city offices where on request he signs his name in beautiful copperplate writing. Over the years he has been distributing pennies to the young children, flattering their parents and imprinting his personality and generosity on all. His investment has proved a brilliant success.

'The Galloping Major' appeared on the scene some years ago. Dressed in a fawn military-type coat, he marched briskly along the streets, pacing himself:

Hup, hup, left right, left right.

Young boys soon realized the possibilities and shouted military commands to him, and his response was immediate, coming to attention, pivoting, and setting off again at the quick march.

In the days before the advent of television and the resurgence of ballad sessions in the pubs, the cinema shared with the dance halls a monopoly of entertainment. It was necessary to queue for long periods to gain admission and the local balladeers found a ready audience who welcomed any diversion to while away the waiting time. Another Cork character who in his younger days was inclined to remove his shoes and deposit them in the confession boxes in St Peter and Paul's Church in order to solicit more sympathy, sang his own version of the ballads. It wasn't that he was particularly talented in the fields of composition but that he usually picked up the words incorrectly and songs like his favourite, 'The Valley of Knockenure' finished 'And they shot them in pairs, coming down the stairs in the Valley of Knockenure'. His commentaries on current affairs and prominent personalities were often pungent, and on occasions when he had failed to ascertain the identity of the listeners retribution was often swift and painful.

Jerry Bruton was another of the queue performers Jerry played the mouth-organ and sang, as far as can be ascertained his one and only song, 'Lets all go down the Marina'. Jerry was a gentle, inoffensive person. On one occasion he was entertaining the patrons of the 'Le Chateau' in Patrick's Street. It is a long bar with a side entrance from Academy Street and Jerry had commenced his recital at the entrance moving slowly down the length of the bar. Halfway down he encountered another mendicant. They saluted gravely, one professional to another, and each went his way. It was only later that Jerry discovered that his colleague had made a collection on the strength of Jerry' performance. He laughed and ordered a pint.

While the increasing standard of living was shepherding in the demise of the cinema as the mass medium of entertainment it was also providing an opportunity for some people to earn a bit more money. The density of traffic on the roads was substantial, and one of the problems created was the provision and maintenance of car parks. One family took it upon themselves to be the guardians of one particular area of the city which was used extensively for car-parking. They ushered motorists in and out of the parking areas and naturally expected a gift for their services. The coloquialism to describe this type of activity is a 'touch'. The father had a very close attachment to his family, and it is reported that when one of the sons married the father granted him sole rights to Patrick St as his touching area. This attachment also manifested itself in another direction for when another member died the father presented each of the mourners with a lock of hair of the dead boys head.

On one occasion when father and son were temporarily

financially embarrased and both were anxious to have a pint they entered Billy Mackessy's pub in Oliver Plunkett St. Billy Mackessy, a noted athlete in his young days and the possessor of All Ireland medals in both hurling and football was approached at one end of the counter by the father. The son took his position at the far end of the bar.

'Mr Mackessy' said the father 'I was arguing with the son there this morning and he doesn't believe that you won two All Ireland medals in hurling and football with Cork. Aren't I right, Mr Mackessy?'

'You're right all right,' says Billy Mackessy, 'I did.'

'That's what I told him, Mr Mackessy,' said the father, 'but you know these young fellows, you have a couple yourself, you can't tell them anything!' and the father trots off to rejoin his son at the far end of the bar. He summoned the barman: 'Mr Mackessy said to give us two pints.'

'Who are you trying to cod now?' said the barman who knew his two clients well.

'He did, he did' said the father and, attracting the attention of Billy Mackessy at the far end of the bar, he calls out: 'Mr Mackessy, Mr Mackessy, wasn't it two you said, two?'

And Billy Mackessy, obviously wanting to extricate himself from the argument between father and son replied, 'That's right "two".'

The father turned to the barman: 'There, now, what did I tell you. Didn't I say "two"?

They got their drink!

Seated on the window-sill of a solicitors office in the South Mall, a gentleman with a legal bent dispensed advice free gratis. Although he was not a qualified lawyer it was generally agreed that his advice was of a high standard and substantially accurate. The solicitors, concerned that his presence was either an embarrassment, or worse again, that prospective clients were availing of his services in preference to theirs, decided to take action. They had a set of spikes inserted on the window-sill thereby depriving him of his position. It was a subtle and grevious blow, a sore point. However all was not lost and an engineer from an office across the street, sympathetic to the benevolent old gentleman and concerned that free legal advice should be available to the citizenry, came to the rescue. Having measured the window-sill and the position of the spikes he constructed an ingenious wooden seat which fitted snugly over the spikes and yet afforded a comfortable seat. Business continued as usual.

One of the most prominent private citizens ever to have lived in Cork was the late Mr Dan Hobbs. He was a prominent member of the business community who spent most of free time organizing and participating in the various charitable functions in the city. Danny's speciality was in organizing variety concerts in which he often contributed himself, singing a comic song, 'The little shirt me mother made for me.' He was a keen sportsman, a follower of 'The Barrs' and Cork hurling teams and he supported his own pack of foot-beagles. His motor car had a distinctive registration number, ZF I, to which Danny had installed a special horn which gave out a hunting call when Danny wished to salute fellow huntsmen in the streets. On one occasion when Danny stopped in town to give that other great character, the late Cissy Young, a lift home, he found that she was having trouble getting into the car. Cissie was a big woman and at this time troubled by arthritis. Eventually Danny commented: 'Cissy, girl, I know the number is ZF but in this case it is AIF, arse in first.' When Danny was seriously ill, he commented to a visitor: 'You know it would be just my luck to die on a Friday and be buried on a Sunday when all the boys will be at the Munster Final in Limerick and they won't be able to go to my funeral.' And so it was.

Another great supporter of the 'Barrs' hurling team was the late 'Leather' Dick Barry. The nickname arose from the fact that Dick worked most of his life in a leather shop. Dick's function in the Club was to take care of the gear, something which he did with as great care as if the jerseys were his own. Once when the 'Barrs' were playing, the referee, whose jersey was almost identical with the opponents' was advised to approach Dick who possibly would have a spare jersey. He explained his predicament to Dick who immediately handed the referee a blue jersey of the 'Barrs.'

The referee explained that this was not the answer to his problem that he could not referee the game in the colours of one of the participating teams, did Dick have a different coloured jersey? 'I don't know any other colour!' was Dick's comment.

There was the gentleman from the South side who was accustomed to have a few drinks on a Friday night and on his way home in the evening stood in the middle of the street 'My name is ... I'm a hurler, a bowl-player and a man and I can puck a sliotar from here over Queen's College.'

And there was the man from Blackpool who became the street cranky in his drink and would regularly go out into the street and challenge any man to come out and fight: 'I can beat any man, big or small, young or old. Come out and fight, I'm not afraid of anyone. I've died once before for Ireland and I'm not afraid to die again!'

'Tom Pepper', another resident of Blackpool, was once to comment in the course of an argument, on the advisability or otherwise of beards: 'Sure Jesus Christ, the Lord have mercy on Him, had a beard too!'

If not inevitable, it was at least understandable that some of these characters should be tempted into the limelight of public life. What is surprising is that so many did in fact offer themselves for election, and most surprising of all, some in fact were elected. Besides John W. Reidy, Jerry Bruton was unsuccesssful, and another who offered himself, and again unfortunately unsuccessful, was Jerry McCarthy. Alias 'The Rancher', Jeremiah was a self-employed worker. He sold bundles of firewood and pushing his box-car around the city he was a familiar sight, in the streets. When the spirit moved him he was inclined to demonstrate his prowess in military exercises. Throwing himself down on the ground, he inched his way along the ground, pausing now and then to machine-gun his enemies. On rising he made a speech before going on his way. A short time later he would repeat the manoeuvre. On one occasion a visiting American tourist, witnessing the procedure and naturally intrigued as he had failed entirely to understand the Rancher's

43

harangue, asked his neighbour to explain. He was perplexed when the second person spoke in an accent which he failed entirely to decipher. It was the ubiquitous gentleman with the speech defect already referred to.

The 'Rancher' in his campaign expected a volume of support from the suburb of Blackpool, the home of Glen Rovers hurling Club of which the 'Rancher' was a keen and devoted follower. The support did not materialize and the 'Rancher' was bitterly disappointed. Shortly afterwards, a poem attributed to the 'Rancher' and titled 'The Ranchers Curse' was circulated in the city. His rancour against the Glen who had just completed an unprecedented and unequalled run of nine un-interrupted victories in the Cork senior hurling championship impregnated the poem and included lines like:

'Nine Counties won but never again
Up the Barrs and F ... the Glen.'

'Dr' Healy appeared on the public face of the city in the 1920s. It was generally believed that he enjoyed a disability pension from the British Government having been shell-shocked in the first World War. His garb was rather eccentric: bowler hat, winged shirt collars, silk waist coat, swallow tailed coat, pepper and salt plus fours and pats. He was affectionately known as the 'Dyker', 'Klondyke', and 'Doctor'. His military achievements were rather vague; over the years his claims, ranging from pilot to anti-aircraft gunner to ship's captain, successfully obscuring the true position. He claimed to have dug for gold in the Yukon, a claim which was no doubt the basis for his nickname 'the Dyker'. He was a gentle little man, courteous to the extreme of lifting his hat even to young children who saluted him in the streets as Doctor and replying 'Good Morning, Sir'. A devout Catholic, he was once incensed when a photographer executed a clever montage and distributed a photograph showing the 'Dyker' shaking hands with Joe Stalin.

The title of doctor was conferred by the students during a rag-week and the ceremony was performed on top of one of the old war time air raid shelters. There was buckets of 'blood' for colour and later 'The Dyker' was ceremoniously dumped in the river. It was the college students who impressed on the 'Dyker' his responsibilities to the community and insisted that he should seek election to the Corporation. They guaranteed that they would meet the financial commitments and organize the campaign.

Dr Healy spoke outside churches, after masses, confraternaties and devotions, but his favourite rostrum was from the steps of the Green Door restaurant at the junction of Patrick's Street and Academy Street. His rostrum was complete with table and chairs, jug and glass of water, usually laced with a heavy dose of Epsom salts, and quite often the 'Dyker' was compelled to adjourn his meetings and answer the call of nature. A regular attender at his meetings was the City Manager for whom the 'Dyker' had a most uncharacteristic and unChristian antipathy. He railed against the manager, but he was always circumspect referring to him as a 'certain city manager in this city'.

The principal plank in the 'Dykers' campaign was that a toilet should be erected for the ladies in the centre of the city. He was incensed that a public convenience was not then at their disposal. Was this not discrimination of a dastardly nature? Were not the women of Cork not also flesh and blood? 'Europe is in a turmoil. We are poised on the brink of a second world war. The nations of Europe are frantically rearming. They are spending millions of pounds on arsenals – and all I ask is one urinal'. He was elected to the Corporation and in due course the ladies toilet was erected on Lavitt's Quay, opposite the Opera house. The 'Dyker', captivated by his success, approached the city manager and requested that his portrait be hung in the porch. The manager is said to have expressed his disappointment that this could not be done but suggested that, as an alternative the 'Dyker's' portrait be printed on the toilet paper!

Besides attracting the recognizable characters, politics also produced a spate of malapropisms and spoonerisms and nicknames. An old campaigner, a Mr Daly earned himself the title 'due course' from his perpetually assuring the people that their problems would be attended to 'in due course.' A recent campaigner, assuring the people that only strong government could handle the gigantic problems of the present, that coalition government was ineffective, that once before it had mis-led the people, stated the people had already 'been mis-led by the coalition'. On another occasion, when challenged for his opinion of the Common Market, he assured the questioner that it was receiving his attention. 'I was down the Coal Quay this morning and the place was filthy and I guarantee to have it cleaned up next week'. Some years ago a speaker, attacking the government for their inability to halt emigration and their failure to increase employment, said that 'it was a terrible shame to see the ships walking round the streets and the men tied up at the docks idle!'

H.V. Morton in his book *In Search of Ireland* commented that the Cork people stay up all night thinking up aphorisms to entertain their friends the following night! But 'slagging', the art of badinage, in an integral part of city life and find its expressions in the cinemas, at games, but not unfortunately anymore in the theatres where respectability now holds sway, and while one is expected to applaud performances, the equal right of showing disapproval is not permitted. The 'Gods' the upper balcony in the Savoy cinema was, in its time, before the advent of television, the Mecca of all slaggers. It probably reached the zenith of its power and expression only shortly before the attendances began to wane and the sanctuary of anonymity was lost. Lux toilet soap must have expended a considerable amount of money on a particular colourful advertisement. The unctious voice of the salesmen was extolling its virtues, 'We have pink Lux, blue Lux, white Lux' when the stage whisper came thundering down from the 'Gods' 'And Bollux!' It was repeated a few nights later in another cinema and the advertisement was then withdrawn.

Nick-names have been accepted as part and parcel of life, come down one generation to the next, in many cases accepted without rancour. Some of the nicknames extend beyond one particular family, embracing all the families of the same name – the Walloo Dunleas, the Wacker Murphys etc. Individual nick-names are christened out of some particular incident and many stick for the person's lifetime. 'The Golden Boy', 'The Glassy Boy', 'Bolshoi', there are literally thousands in the city.

While many of the old names of the streets have been changed over the years from their original English to the more appropriate ones of Irish connotation, the naming of the streets in the new suburbs show an interesting feature. Indeed it is possible to date the various estates without any reference to the city records. The Catholic Church celebrated the Marian Year and numerous streets bear witness of this occasion and there are Marian Estates, Terraces, Square, Crescents all over the city. Similarly the practice of naming houses, the bane of a postman's life, indicates the date of building or purchase. Thus the papal names Pacellis and Roncallis — denote their date of construction, The naming of houses affords the occupier a greater opportunity to display ingenuity or perversity. The most common of all the names are those of a religious nature and denote little else but the denomination of the resident. There are however, the names which indicate the origin of the people: the Ballinacarrigas, the Toames, the Keimcorabullas, for it seems that many people cannot fail but admit their origin to the world. Ingenuity is a truly rare gift and many people, thinking themselves to be its possessor conceive the most plebian of anagrams Larkit, Larry and Kitty; Chrisdoney, Christine and Donal, etc. A romantic interlude may influence others and many the house has been called after the honeymoon haven of a couple. On occasions this may prove an embarrasment as was the case of the couple who having spent their honeymoon in Spain called their house Bordello only to have the student of Spanish inform them of its proper meaning.

CHAPTER 6

St Finnbarr's Cemetery, situated in the village of Glasheen, is the largest of the Municipal graveyards. It is an interdenominational graveyard but even in death the religions are segregated, for the Protestants are interned in one section and the Catholics in the other.

Located immediately inside the main gateway, the Republican Plot is reserved for all those who were active in the War of Independence. It is circumscribed by a low granite wall and dominated by a large cross, designed by Seamus Murphy R.H.A. The motif on the cross, a two-handed Irish sword, is based on a sword dredged up out of the river Suir. Although the sword was then incomplete, being broken off near the hilt, experts reconstructed it. It is a fine example of this type of ancient Irish weapon. This cross was commissioned by a committee formed by the various Republican groups in the city, apparently on the understanding that it would be unveiled by prominent local veterans of the 'Troubles'. Shortly before the official opening it was decided to ask the President Mr DeValera, to perform the function, a decision which did not meet with the approval of several of the interested bodies. The night previous to the official opening, some members of the I.R.A. entered the graveyard and attempted to blow up the monument. In a premature explosion one young man was killed and a second seriously injured although the cross suffered but superficial damage. Civil proceedings were not preferred.

Mr DeValera is one of the most controversial figures in modern Irish history. His birth in Brooklyn saved him from execution after the 1916 Rising when his wife, the beloved Sinead, requested the American President, Wilson to intercede. Mr DeValera, one of the few senior commanders to survive the executions, quickly rose to a pre-eminent position in the Freedom Movement. Following the War of Independence and the signing of the Treaty, the Republican forces split in two factions, those under Michael Collins who favoured the acceptance of the Treaty and those under Eamonn DeValera who opposed it. The Treaty was subsequently ratified by Parliament and at the polls. One of the most contentious items was the provision whereby the elected members of Parliament were required to swear an oath of allegiance to the British Crown – a condition which Mr DeValera found unacceptable. The Civil War followed until peace was eventually restored, and in 1926 Mr DeValera founded the Fianna Fail Party and in 1927 he entered Parliament and took the oath of allegiance, or as the then termed it 'an empty formula'. One wonders what circumstances caused the 'oath of allegiance' of 1922 to subsequently become 'an empty formula'.

The influence which Mr DeValera wielded over the Irish people throughout the long years of his leadership is now difficult to appreciate but was analogous to that of the Papacy, being in the light of DeValera's power and influence both temporal and spiritual. And yet, his contribution to the cause of the revival of the Gaelic language, a movement to which he expressed un-equivocal support is – to say the least – uninspiring.

The graves of two of Cork's cherished and respected men lie within the walls of the Republican Plot: Terence MacSwiney and Tomás MacCurtáin. Tomás MacCurtáin, the first Republican Lord Mayor of the city, lived in Blackpool. On the night of the 20 March 1920, a squad of 'seirbhisig Gall' (servants of the English) raided the house and in the presence of his wife and young family, shot him dead. The coroner's inquest returned the most remarkable and courageous verdicts in history. As published in the newspapers of 17 April 1920 it read:

We find that the late Ald. Thomas MacCurtain, Lord Mayor of Cork, died from shock and haemorrhage, caused by bullet wounds, and that he was wilfully murdered under circumstances of the most callous brutality, and that the murder was organized and carried out by the

Royal Irish Constabularly, officially directed by the British Government, and we return a verdict of wilful murder against David Lloyd George, Prime Minister of England; Lord French, Lord Lieutenant of Ireland; Ian Macpherson, late chief Secretary of Ireland; Acting Inspector-General Smith of the Royal Irish Constabularly; Divisional Inspector Clayton of the Royal Irish Constabularly; District Inspector Swanzy, and some unknown members of the Royal Irish Constabularly. We strongly condemn the system at present in vogue, of carrying out raids at unreasonable hours. We tender to Mrs MacCurtain and family our sincerest sympathy in their terrible bereavement, this sympathy we extend to the citizens of Cork in the loss they sustained by the death of one eminently capable of directing their civic administration.

Terence MacSwiney, teacher, newspaper editor, and author, succeeded Tomás MacCurtáin to the mayoralty.

On 12 August 1920 the City Hall was surrounded by soldiers, Lord Mayor MacSwiney was arrested, tried by court-martial and sentenced to two years imprisonment. As a protest against this seizing of the Chief Magistrate of the City, he immediately went on hunger strike. He was taken by warship to London and interned in Brixton Prison. After a fast of seventy-four days, and the rumoured application of forced feeding, he died. The British Government, fearing a great reception and demonstration in Dublin, seized the corpse at Holyhead, and unaccompanied by relatives sent it under strong military guard to Cork. Despite these precautions a Guard of Honour was mounted over the coffin on the sea journey by a detachment of his colleagues.

His protest evoked widespread interest and sympathy throughout the world and contributed largely to the cause of the Republican movement. An indication of this influence may be the story of the aged American lady, herself with no Irish connections, who remembered him when she was a young child. 'Gee, now I remember him. I was a very young girl and we had a cat that we called MacSwiney because it wouldn't eat!'

Next to the graves of MacCurtáin and MacSwiney lies that of Denis Barry. He was a victim of the Civil War and like MacSwiney died on hunger strike in Portlaois Prison. His body was returned to Cork. But in accordance with the directives of the Catholic Bishop the parish priests in both the North and South Chapels refused to permit the body to rest overnight in either of the churches. Eventually it lay in state in the upper floor of the bow-fronted house adjoining the city library in the Grand Parade. All day long thousands of citizens, defied the edict of the Bishop and paraded past. Another victim of the struggle for independence, who also lies in the Republican Plot, is Joe Murphy who died of hunger strike in Cork Gaol after a fast of ninety-two days.

The building now occupied by Donnelly's school in Glasheen village was previously the home of the Sheares family. It was their 'country home' although it was but one and a half miles from the city centre. Their city home was in Sheares Street. The family was a wealthy and respected one, being prominent bankers in the city in the eighteenth century. The brothers were very much influenced by the French revolution, they visited France and indeed were present at the execution of Marie Antoinette. They shared the same boat as Daniel O'Connell, on their return, and he tore the cockades from their hats as soon as the boat had left the harbour. Betrayed like most of the United Irishmen, they were executed.

There are three main arteries leading from the western suburbs into the city: the Glasheen, Magazine, and College Roads. University College Cork is situated on the latter. It is a beautiful building, built in the Gothic style and designed by Sir Thomas Deane in 1848. Macauley was to say of it that it would have done credit to Oxford, and it may be more than coincidence that Sir Thomas Deane did in fact borrow from the Cork builder Mr Hill, many of his sketches of Oxford. Under the terms of the Universities Act of 1908 the name was changed from the original Queen's College to the present University College, Cork. The Honan Hostel attached to the University was a gift to the University from the Honan family, as was the college chapel, the Honan

Chapel. The Irish Universities Act precludes the expenditure of College funds for the expenditure or maintenance of any church, chapel or other place of religious worship or service, and the executors of Isabella Honan's will, decided to erect a church for the use of the hostel residents and for 'the scholars and students of Munster'.

The chapel is the work of James F. McMullen, architect, the builder was John Sisk and Son, and the foundation stone was laid 18 May 1915 by the Most Reverend Thomas A O'Callaghan, D.D., Bishop of Cork. It is of interest that the architect and builder were both Corkman and the stonework was executed by the local firm of Henry Emery and his workmen, Cork.

Contrary to local opinion the chapel is not a replica of Cormac's Chapel on the Rock of Cashel, and its dimensions of nave and chancel at 72 feet × 28 feet, and 26 feet × 18 feet, respectively are almost twice that of Cormac's Chapel. Possibly the single most pronounced influence is that of St Cronan's Church, Roscrea. The church is, rather, representative of the complete picture of hiberno-romanesque style of architecture. It is complete to the round tower at the north-east corner, the very distinctive feature of the early Irish monastic scene.

The main entrance, in the west gable and modelled on that of St Cronan's church, is built in three orders, each differently decorated. Surmounting the doorway is a triangular pediment and an image of St Finnbarr executed by Oliver Sheppard R.H.A., is contained within the tympanum. The church is built in uncoursed, squared rubble masonry in the grey-white limestone of Cork.

While the interior contains many intricate carvings, brilliantly decorated stained glass-windows and 'stations', the overall impression is that of dignity and simplicity. The mosaic floor is a particularly beautiful one. At the entrance, a great beast is depicted and from its mouth a torrent of water flows up the centre aisle. In the water a multitude of fish and monsters are represented, and in front of the sanctuary the waters divide and a beast half serpent, half whale, basks on the surface. To right and left animals drink from

52

the stream, representative of The Water of Life. Within the sanctuary all the elements are depicted, the galaxy, wind, rain, fire, water, mountains, and plains, and all things created. The complete design is circumscribed by a border of intricate interlacing and the little beasts so beloved of the early Celtic scribes.

In the sanctuary, the altar table, a plain slab of limestone, is supported by simply carved legs, each bearing a different form of Irish crucifixion representation and the tabernacle is made in shape of an ancient Irish Church. The doors and tympanum of the tabernacle are a brilliant pattern of enamel.

The stations of the Cross, executed in Opus Sectile are some of the most beautiful ever executed in this medium. There are nineteen stained-glass windows, eleven of which were executed by Harry Clarke, and the remainder by Sarah Purser R.H.A. and the two distinct styles are evident. Harry Clarke's windows are a blaze of rich deep colours, the figures, in the Celtic tradition; Miss Purser's are a combination of pale tints and a naturalistic representation of form. The outstanding work is the east window, the work of John Child, and depicts the risen Christ. The windows in the nave represent the Irish saints Ita, Colman, Brendan, Gobnait, Flannan, Carthage, Patrick, Brigid, Colmcille, Munchin, Fachtna, Ailbe, Albert, and Finnbarr.

The Celtic influence is complete even to the gold chalice and ciborium, the intricately worked leather covers on the missals, the tapestries behind the altar and the vestments. The chasuble in particular, is after the design of the draperies depicted on the ancient Celtic Crosses. The Processional Cross is a replica of the Cross of Cong and the panels are decorated with gold filagree work, jewels, and studs of enamel.

In all the Honan Chapel is a brilliant reconstruction of the hiberno-romanesque style of architecture.

The private homes of the British Army Officers stationed in Cork were formerly situated in Wellington Square, Magazine Road. Magazine Road itself was so called because of an old military magazine which stood there.

The Lough of Cork is a large lake with two islands in its

centre. It is a wonderful natural amenity in the centre of an extensive residential area and for years has been a favourite haunt of children and adults alike who fish for coarse fish, perch, and roach, as well as the tiny minnows, 'tawrneens' in the patois. The fishing tackle is rudimentary: a bamboo pole and a length of line for roach and a length of thread with a worm tied to it for the minnows. Some years ago English anglers discovered it and their display of equipment, deck-chairs, etc., was a great source of amusement to the locals. It is also the centre for the playing of the local street leagues in hurling and football. In the eighteenth century the city was granted a charter permitting the holding of fairs during the summer months at the Lough but this privilege has not been availed of for many years. The Lough is also a bird sanctuary; a flock of Canada geese was introduced and now breed there every year. As is to be expected the Lough abounds in legend and folklore and the story is that under the island there is a fairy fort. At the wedding of a daughter of the house, the young girl was permitted to visit the well to obtain a glass of water but she forgot to lock the door so that the water overflowed and the castle and all the residents were submerged in the waters.

Daniel Corkery wrote his book *The Threshold of Quiet* on the shores of the Lough. On one occasion when visited by Patrick Pearse they spent many hours talking by the lake-side. This was in the days before the path and protecting wall had been built and it seems that Pearse had been upset by the sound of the waters lapping against the shore for as he was leaving he commented to Corkery, 'Why don't you get at the Corporation to do something about that and get them to drain it!' Daniel Corkery was appalled.

The Corporation housing estate of Ballyphehane is one of the largest and most successful projects in the city. Although it suffers the usual weakness of uniformity of colour and design, it is well planned; wide roads flanked by lines of cherry trees which bloom a glorious pink in spring, lawns, and flower beds; the houses arranged in squares, crescents, and semi-circles; schools, and one of the most successful credit unions in the country. It incorporates the old village communities of Pouladuff and Togher and approximates to some extent to the ideal of a mixed community. It stretches from the Lough to the junction of the Kinsale Road.

To the east of the Kinsale Road, at Frankfield, Sir Henry Brown Hayes, one of the most interesting, if infamous, characters lived in Vernon Mount. The house, now in the possession of the Munster Motor Cycle and Car Club, is an unusual building decorated with weird frescoes and the reputation of having a 'priests' room' although this has never been found. Sir Henry Brown Hayes was of a wealthy Cork family. A city sherriff at the age of nineteen, a Freeman of the city at twenty one, he was probably the most notorious of 'The Young Bucks Society', who terrorized the countryside at the turn of the nineteenth century. He was a commissioned officer in the South Cork Militia and while in the field was accustomed to pitch a silken canopy over his tent. When it was fashionable to wear a cockade at the side of the hat Hayes wore one — at either side.

At this particular time, the 1820s, the family fortunes were rather low and Hayes, then a widower and forty years of age, decided to marry into money and replenish the coffers. His choice of spouse was Mary Pike, the daughter and heir to the fortune of the wealthy banking family. When Mary Pike was visiting friends a messenger arrived at the house asking her to return home immediately, that her mother was ill. She took her departure immediately only to discover that the messenger was none other than the sister of Henry Brown Hayes. She was then informed that Sir Henry had decided to marry her. On her refusal Hayes himself appeared to plead his case and when Miss Pike obstinately refused to marry him, he took her to his house at Vernon Mount, detained her against her wishes, and informed that she would remain there until she consented. Miss Pike, however, refused to be intimidated and persisted in her refusal. The following day Hayes introduced a 'clergyman' who performed a 'marriage' ceremony. Her continued refusal to accept the validity of the ceremony eventually wore down Sir Henry's resolve and eventually she was released.

Miss Pike reported her abduction to the authorities who placed a reward of £500 on his head. Miss Pike added a further £500 to the amount of the reward. His arrest inevitable, Sir Henry conspired with a friend, Coughlan, a hairdresser, in the grand Parade, and arranged to be arrested in his custody. Coughlan collected the £1000 reward and subsequently erected three red-bricked houses on the Grand Parade, the rents from these enabling him to live.

Miss Pike, a Quaker, unable to institute legal proceedings, renounced the Society of Friends (which she later rejoined). The prosecuting attorney was John Philpott Curran. The trial caused a sensation and crowds gathered to witness it. Curran on approaching the Courthouse was greeted with the salutation 'Good luck your honour, may you win the day!'

To which he replied

If I do you will lose your knight.

The trial was even the subject of a popular ballad

Sir Henry kissed behind the bush,
Sir Henry, kissed a Quaker,
And if he did, the dirty thing
I'm sure he did not ate her.

Sir Henry Brown Hayes, tried and convicted, was sentenced to death, but this was subsequently commuted to life banishment to Australia. On his outward journey Hayes, availing of the practise of the day, was able to bribe his way to preferential treatment, a fact which caused much resentment on board the ship. On arrival in Australia he settled in Sydney.

Inconvenienced by the reptiles he subsequently sent a ship home to Ireland, commissioned to return with a cargo of Irish turf, apparently subscribing to the piseog that as St Patrick had banished all the snakes and reptiles out of Ireland they could not survive on Irish soil. Eventually his daughter having struck up an acquaintenance with the Prince of Wales, succeeded in having his sentence commuted, and Sir Henry Brown Hayes set sail once more for Ireland. On his journey homeward his ship was wrecked but he survived the catastrophe and he landed safely in Cobh in yellow trousers and two cockades on his hat. He died in Grattan Hill, and although a certain doubt exists as to his final resting place it is now accepted that he is buried in Christ Church, South Main Street.

CHAPTER 7

The Church of Christ the King, Turner's Cross, is one of
the architectural sights of the city. It was designed by the
Irish-American architect Barry Byrne, who died in 1969,
and completed and blessed for Divine service by Bishop Coholan, 25 October 1931. In its time it was the
cause of much speculation and controversy. It was the first
mass-concrete building in the city and the cause of industrial unrest, the stonemasons, seeing in it a grievous blow
against their age old craft, contested its construction fiercely
but in the last analysis tradition gave way to progress and
the construction progressed. It was originally designed for
an American architectural competition and was placed second before it was eventually commissioned for Turner's
Cross. It is a magnificent building in the modern manner,
simple almost to the point of austerity, its width exceeds the
length by sixteen feet. From a fan-lighted apex the roof de-
scends in step-like grace to the comparatively low side
walls. There are no pillars. The only ornamentation are the
stations of the cross which were executed by Egans of Patrick Street. The mosaic extending the full length of the
centre aisle corresponds to the geometric pattern of the
church. The modern stained-glass windows, complimenting
the south or main entrance of the church recede from the
high altar in direct proportion to the main front walls of the
church. The figure of Christ at the front door was designed
by the American sculptor John Storr and executed by John
Maguire of Cork.

The Augustinian Friary, known as the Red Abbey, lies
off Douglas Street. There is a certain confusion as to its
foundation, Smith in his history ascribing it to the fifteenth
century. It would appear, however, that this date refers to
the building of the present structure as other documents indicate a much older establishment on this site-probably as

early as the twelfth century. The monastery was an extensive establishment, possessing fishing rights on the river and a substantial tract of land on which the City Hall is now built. The lands stretched as far west as the present Friar's Walk. For many years a hospital of the Knights Hopitalers of St John of Jerusalem was near the Friary. In 1690 the Duke of Marlborough directed the siege of the city from the tower. It was this siege which effectively saw the end of the city walls for after that they were allowed to fall into ruin, and over the years the stone was used as building material. The Duke of Grafton was killed during the siege, probably near the South Mall.

During the siege Marlborough threatened to raze the 'new suburbs', now known as French's Quay, but agreed to stay his hand on payment of a fine of £500. The money was duly handed over by the city merchants but Marlborough subsequently burned the district to the ground. The Friary buildings were confiscated after the Reformation and in the following centuries saw many changes of ownership. The buildings gradually fell into disrepair, and at present only the ruins of the tower remain as are reminder of this once important monastic settlement.

In 1880 when construction work was being carried out in Douglas Street tunnels which appeared to run in the general direction of the Friary were discovered, unfortunately no excavations were conducted and the purpose of these tunnels remains speculative.

The Catholic Church of St Finnbarr's South near the Red Abbey is the fourth church to stand in this locality. The first church built since the Reformation was probably in Cat Lane and was erected in the first half of the seventeenth century. A second church, a thatched building stood in Douglas Street but this was destroyed by fire, in 1728. The third church was erected in the same year and in 1731 was described as 'a slated mass house in the south suburbs'. In 1766 the present building was erected. It is in the Georgian style and it is not known now if the North Transept was erected at the same time but the South Transept was added in 1809 and is not in proportion to the rest of the building. The altar contains 'The Dead Christ' by Hogan, and the Crucifixion behind the altar is reputed to be the work of the Cork artist John O'Keeffe.

At the South Gate Bridge, Barrack Street begins its narrow twisting climb up the slopes on the south side of the city. This street was formerly the main entry and exit route to the city from the west. It is one of the oldest districts built outside the walls and in its time was one of the principal commercial areas in the city. It was up to comparatively recent times a densely populated area, small lanes running off the Barrack Street to the south and north. A distinctive feature of the street is the proliferation of hucksters shops and public houses, which still survive despite the competion of supermarkets, and chain stores. Alongside the Brown Derby public house is the site of the old Apple Market, and up to the 1920s the apple growers from all over the county brought their 'kishes', large baskets of apples, into this market and offered them for sale.

Many of the shops had unusual occupations and near the Apple Market one shop specialized in the manufacture and sale of nails which in those days had to be made by hand.

The 'Gateway' public house lays claim to being the oldest licensed premises in the country, and boasts of being founded in 1689. Over the years it has had some notable clients, The Duke of Wellington and Diarmuid O'Donovan Rossa among them. Rossa was a man of legendary will and strength of character who survived a long period of imprisonment and lived to write his story. He was committed for his part in the Fenian Rising of 1867 and after his release he worked in America editing the Fenian newspaper. It was at his funeral that Patrick Pearse spoke the now celebrated oration which committed the I.R.B. to another attempt at rebellion and concludes:

'But the fools, the fools, the fools they have left us our Fenian dead. And while Ireland holds these graves, Ireland, unfree, shall never be at peace.'

Pearse, poet, playwright, essayist, and schoolteacher was in 1916 to lead the Rising and be executed together with his brother .

60

On 24 November 1904, O'Donovan Rossa was elected a Freeman of the city, 'As a tribute to his many sterling qualities as an Irish Nationalist, and as one who has suffered a long term of penal servitude for his devotion to the cause of Ireland.'

One of the darkest blots on Cork pride concerns another Freeman, the great Celtic Scholar, the German, Kuno Meyer. In 1915, the loyalist members of the Cork Corporation had his name expunged from the list of Freeman. That this decision was rescinded on 14 May 1920 reflects the changing pattern of these times.

The custom of awarding the 'Freedom of the City' to distinguished people in recognition of their public service dates back to the fourteenth century. However, the burning of the Court House and the destruction of the documents have resulted in the loss of the complete list of Freemen, but among those elected were Dean Swift and Captain Richard Roberts who navigated the *Sirius* the first steamship to cross the Atlantic from Europe, Cobh to New York in 1938. Among the other Freemen were Charles Stewart Parnell, Gladstone, John Redmond, Andrew Carnegie (as an acknowledgement of the munificent donation of £10,000 to Cork for the erection of a Free Library.) Douglas Hyde (in recognition of his invaluable services towards the revival of the Irish language), Edward O'Meagher Condon, Captain of the 69th regiment U.S. Army., An t-Athair Peadar O Laoire (in recognition of his priceless services to the Irish Language and to the Irish Literary Movement generally.), Very Rev. Father Thomas Dowling O.S.F.C. Guardian Holy Trinity Church Cork (for his services in preserving the peace of the city by his successful adjustment of industrial disputes.) Woodrow Wilson; Dr Mannix, Archbishop of Melbourne; Rev. Father Dominick O.S.F.C. (as a mark of respect for his valuable services rendered as Chaplain to the first two Republican Lord Mayors of Cork, and especially for his steadfast devotion to the late Terence MacSwiney T.D. while he was suffering and dying for his country in Brixton Prison, and as a mark of appreciation of his own suffering in Ireland's cause.) Sir Frank Benson, the actor; Sean T.O'Kelly, President of Ireland; Cardinals D'Alton, Cushing, Browne and Conway; John F. Kennedy, President of America.

Alongside the 'Gateway' are the ruins of Elizabeth Fort. This fortress built on a limestone outcrop of rock was constructed to remind the citizens of the city's vulnerability to cannonade and to ensure the containment of their rebellious inclinations. Elizabeth Fort was razed by the citizens in 1603 but they were compelled to rebuild it at their own expense. In 1835 it was used as a female convict prison and later it reverted to military use and later handed over to the Irish State. In August 1922, during the course of the Civil War, the fort was destroyed by fire and now only the outer fortifications remain.

Barrack Street is a part of the city now undergoing a major change. Formerly a densely populated district, a labyrinth of narrow laneways, lined by tiny houses, led off the main thoroughfare but many of these have been levelled and are being replaced by Corporation housing estates. It is an area rich in tradition, tracing its history back to the coming of St Finnbarr and the construction of his monastery in Gill Abbey. It is the home of St Finnbarr's Hurling and Football Club, which was established in 1876, before the foundation of the Gaelic Athletic Association. It is the home ground of the Barrack Street Band. The 'Barracka' competed in London for the championship of the 'British' Isles and were successful. The members were informed that Queen Victoria would present the trophy but it was expected that the band should play the British National Anthem. The band refused and they returned home to Cork, champions, but without the laurels.

It was a great bird-fancying area, the cages with the finches and linnets hanging on the front walls of the houses. After the fall of Parnell, the city was practically split in two, politically; the north side owing allegiance to one faction, the south side paying tribute to the other. The rivalry between the John Redmondites and the Smith O'Brien factions was intense and the city streets were the scene of much brawling whenever the rival factions chanced to meet.

The Fair Lane Fife and Drum Band, preceded by a half dozen big buxon women (of whom it was said that any one could beat two men) were wont to cross the South Gate Bridge as an act of defiance. Whenever the sound of the band was heard crossing the Bridge, the shout went up 'Barracka'! 'Take in your linnets, here's down Fair Lane', and bird cages and children were whisked indoors and the doors bolted against the 'barbarians' of the north side.

Further up Barrack Street is Old Weigh House Lane. Across the street was one of the toll-houses which ringed the city collecting fees on each entry point to the city.

The old name for Green Street was Gallows Green Street, and it was the site of the old public gallows. The laws have over the years been radically changed but in previous centuries their severity was almost unbelievable. The death sentence was imposed for what are now regarded as quite minor crimes: for instance stealing sheep was a capital offense. The executions were a public affair and, if one is to judge from contemporary accounts, were the occasion for a public holiday. Hanging was by all accounts a rather rough and ready affair and many a 'victim' owes his life to the slipshod manner in which they were carried out. There are records of many instances when the 'victims' survived the hanging. On one occasion a tailor named Redmond was to be executed. A great throng had gathered to witness the event, among them a visiting actor. After the hanging the actor took possession of the 'corpse' and applied some form of respiration. The 'corpse' revived and, thanking the actor, headed for the nearest hostelry to celebrate. Later that evening, feeling that he should, once more, offer his gratitude to the actor he sought him out at the theatre. He staggered on stage much to the consternation of the audience, many of whom, it appears, had been witnesses to his execution earlier in the day. The audience panicked, and four people were seriously injured in the stampede. The theatre is now the General Post Office in Oliver Plunket Street. Up to recent years an old spiral staircase was still in position, but it was removed in the course of alterations to the building.

During the controversy which raged around the re-building of Coventry Cathedral in England, the poet John Betjeman advised the modernists that they should visit St Finn Barre's Cathedral which he called 'a gem of a cathedral'. Its three spires dominate, not only the south side, but the whole city. Churches have stood on this site or in close proximity since the time of St Finnbarr himself. At the time of the Reformation the Catholic church was taken over. In 1735 a medieval cathedral was taken down with the exception of an old tower which was incorporated in the new building. During the 1860s it was decided to erect a new cathedral, the site was cleared and work begun. The stone of this old building was stored for many years in Lancaster Quay, where the municipal authority had a yard. Eventually it was acquired at a nominal fee and used for the construction of the Dominican Oratory in Pope's Quay.

The foundation stone of this new cathedral was laid by Bishop John Gregg in 1865 and it was consecrated on St Andrew's Day 1870. In early pointed gothic style it is the work of John Burgess, whose drawings show that he also planned the interior in minute detail. It is a truly magnificent building, the length of which exceeds the width by a third, its length being 162½ feet. The central tower is 240 feet in height, and the two western ones, 180 feet. The west front, in Ballinasloe limestone, is a wonder of stonework and the deeply recessed portals are filled with statuary.

Much of the expense of this work was born by Mr Sharman Crawford who made a gift of £20,000 to defray the cost. The north or Crawford Portal has statues of Saints Philip, Bartholomew, Simon, John the Baptist, Andrew, James the Apostle, Thomas, and Matthias. The south portal is decorated with statues of Saints Mark, Jude, Peter, Paul, James the Lesser, John, and Luke. A figure of Christ flanked by the five wise and five foolish virgins decorates the central portal. Above the central doorway the tympanum shows the Resurrection and the rose window depicts the Last Judgement. The rose window in the east end depicts the Creation. The Golden Angel in the east roof was a gift of the architect and of this, local tradition has it that before the end of the world the angel will blow her trumpet to advise Cork people to prepare for the Day of Judgement. The carillion of bells, a peal of eight in the north west tower, were cast in 1751 by Rudhalls of Gloucester, England.

The walls of the interior are lined with the red marble of Cork. The magnificent lectern of solid brass is decorated with Italian rock crystals and contains profiles of Moses and David. The cannon ball, suspended from a chain behind the main altar was taken from the old tower when it was being taken down and is said to be a relic of the siege of 1690. Under the pulpit a plaque commemorates the tomb of Elizabeth Aldworth, celebrated as the only woman received into the order of Freemasonry. Hiding in the library of Doneraile Court, she overheard the ritual of the order and, in order to preserve secrecy, she was enrolled. The church contains many plaques commemorating the memory of those who died serving in the British forces. One plaque is in memory of the celebrated Dean Babington. The Dean was a victim of the Sinn Fein election. This election, of vital importance to Sinn Fein, was brilliantly organized, impersonation and all forms of electoral irregularities ensuring a shattering victory for Sinn Fein. Many booths opened and were closed again within the hour with a one hundred per cent poll! When the Dean appeared at his polling Station and introduced himself, the presiding officer informed him that he had already voted illiterate two hours previously! The Dean laughed and went his way. The organ was originally built by Messrs Hill of London, England but was extensively rebuilt by T.W. Magahy and Son of Warren Place Cork. It is enclosed in a pit 14 ft deep and measuring 30' × 20'. The console is 60 feet from the pipes and of an unusual construction is reputed to be the only one of its type in the world. Magahy was a most successful organ designer and among the others he built were Shandon in 1883, at a cost of £580; Rincurran Church; the organ in the Church of Ireland Training College, Dublin; and that for the Cork exhibition of 1883 which earned universal approval.

The first house in Cork of the Order of Friars Preachers or Dominicans, was founded in 1229 by the ancestors of the Barrymore family in that part of the city now known as St

Marie's of the Isle. As the name suggests this was one of the islands in the valley of the Lee but it has now been incorporated into the city. At that time it was outside the walled city and probably contributed to the growth of the French's Quay area of the city. According to the Dominican history, it was a magnificent structure and in honour of the founder the community has his equestrian statue cast in bronze installed in the church. This statue survived until the monastery was suppressed in the reign of Henry VIII. The community received a subvention from the treasury; in 1295 it was thirty-five marks. In 1317 a charter was granted permitting the monks and other good citizens free access to the city by the South Gate entrance. A friar of the Cork Convent was Archbishop of Cologne in 1461. The abbey was suppressed in 1544 and the buildings and lands were granted to William Bourman at the annual rent of six shillings and ninepence. The lands included two acres of small gardens, a watermill, half an acre of land, a fishing pool, half a salmon weir, three acres of arable land, ten other acres of arable land, and twenty acres of pasture land. When Perkin Warbeck landed in Passage and succeeded in recruiting the aid of the citizens and Mayor Waters, who later was executed with Warbeck in Tyburn for this indiscretion, he is reputed to have stayed in the Dominican Monastery. Tradition has it that previous to the suppression of the monastery the monks hid the sacred vessels and their place of refuge is still a mystery.

The district still retains its links with scholarship and learning and two schools, the convent of the Sisters of Mercy and the Crawford Municipal Technical School (another gift to the city from Mr Crawford), are functioning.

CHAPTER 8

Of the many river channels which intersected the marsh
lands in the centre of the valley only two remain visible, the
north and south channels. They run parallel from east to
west, separating at the city waterworks and rejoining at the
Custom House in the east. The only avenue of approach to
the city from the south and west was by way of Barrack
Street and eventually over the South Gate Bridge. For purposes of defense the South Gate Bridge was a strategic location and the bridges have always been well fortified, protected by drawbridge, and fortified on the city side of the
south channel. The early bridges were of timber but subsequently they were replaced by stone and the present one
was designed by Coltsman. It is accepted that it was wid-
ened at a later date and indeed an inspection of the under-
side reveals two distinct types of material, the western section having been added. The old city goal was situated at
the city side of the bridge and some of the cells may still be
seen.

The South Main Street is one of the oldest of the city's
streets. Originally it consisted of two separate streets, but
the Danes, it is thought, built a causeway at the junction of
the present street and Castle Street and formed one continu-
ous thoroughfare, from the North Gate Bridge to the South
Gate, a distance of about 700 yards. This was the axis of
the walled city. Narrow laneways, most of them still in existence: Old Post Office Lane, Cockpit Lane, Portney's
Lane, Phillip's Lane ran off this street to the city walls.

The large Tudor-style building of Beamish and Crawford
Brewers was constructed in 1865. The tradition of brewing
goes back probably to the latter half of the seventeenth century or the beginning of the eighteenth, the owner of this
brewery in 1715 being a Mr Allen. The concern came into
the possession of the present owners in 1791 and quickly

expanded. In 1809 Wakefield says that Guinness 'was then only the second brewer in Ireland, Beamish and Crawford of Cork who brewed upwards of 100,000 barrels per year, standing first.' Close by the brewery there stood an old conical tower known as the 'Old Glass-house' where once fine glass blowing was practised. No trace of this building now stands, nor is there any known sample of the craft, although some bottles in the possession of one of the directors may have come from the 'Old Glass House.' Situated on the parapet of the flight of steps leading to the main entrance is a block of limestone, which tradition tells us was originally placed on the South Gate Bridge. In the days when 'traitors' were executed by being hanged, drawn, and quartered and their heads then impaled on a spike, these gruesome objects were exposed to the populace as a warning. It is thought that the spikes were embedded in this limestone block, and even to the present two holes are drilled into this block. The locks on the main gates are the subject of much speculation. One is reputed to have been taken from the gate of the city and the second is an exact replica of it, although so good that it is not now possible to distinguish between them.

Christ Church shares with St Peters the distinction of being the oldest of ecclesiastical sites within the walled city; the charter of James I confirms this. Many churches have been built on this site and after the Reformation when the Corporation was exclusively Protestant it was chosen by them as their offical church and known as 'King's Chapel'. An earlier church is reputed to have been built by the Knights Templars but no trace of it remains. In 1690 a steeple was added to the church, but during the siege of the same year, when many Protestants took shelter within the church, it was extensively damaged by cannon and it had to be taken down in 1716. A new church, the present one, was erected in 1726 to the design of Coltsman. At the western end of the church a tower of 136 feet began to lean over to such an alarming degree that it became necessary to remove it. It was this incident that gave rise to the old Cork expression 'All to one side like Christ Church', which was attributed to fanatics of any attitude. It was then decided to rebuild and in 1825 the design of George Pain was accepted. However the cost was prohibitive and renovations, including the rebuilding of the west front and the repair of the church were made instead. From an exterior point of view, it is an unpretentious structure, the form oblong, 115' long by 60' wide. Inside there is a beautifully pannelled ceiling, supported by twelve Ionic columns of Scagliola.

Edmond Spencer the poet and author of *The Faery Queen* left us this description of the city:

'The spreading Lee, that like an island fayre
Encloseth Corke with it's divided flood.'

is reputed to have married Elizabeth Boyle, in Christ Church.

Elizabeth Boyle was a kinswoman of Sir Richard Boyle, later to be known as the Earl of Cork. After the Battle of Kinsale when the English forces defeated a combined force of the Irish and the Spanish expeditionary force, he left Shandon Castle and, travelling non-stop to England, he was the first to bring the news of the encounter to Queen Elizabeth. Later he purchased much of the grant of land given to Walter Raleigh and then fortified and erected the town of Bandon at a cost of £ 14,000.

The churchyard contains some very old crypts and headstones of the oldest of Cork families. One of them 'The Modest Man' is now in the portico inside the main doorway. A somewhat macabre story is told of one of the wealthy Cork Families. A widow, shortly before her death, had disinherited her son. About a week after the internment the son, entered the vault, presumably to strip the corpse of the valuable jewellery. Having failed to prise the rings from the fingers he preceeded to cut them off. At the first incision the 'corpse' aroused itself. Apparently the woman had been buried while in a state of suspended animation. She was still a young woman and later remarried and bore her husband two children.

Washington Street was formerly one of the courses of the river but the street has been vaulted in the construction of what is now the principal approach to the city from the west. It was known for years that a stream ran under the street but during repair work some years ago a second stream, running under the other was discovered.

Castle Street at the junction of the North and South Main Streets is built over another of the streams reclaimed from the marsh lands. In 1649 when Cromwell's son-in-law, Henry Ireton, led his forces against the city, his passage was made easier when some of the citizens raised a portcullis which guarded the city at this spot. There was also a Fishambles where now the Catholic Young Men's Society have their premises.

One of the oldest and most fashionable streets of the city, Broad Lane, was up to quite recent times situated at the back entrance to the Franciscan Church in the North Main Street. Broad Lane was the widest of the side streets − it was nine feet wide! Across the roadway, Portney's Lane was similarly a very fashionable residential street and after the disastrous Battle of Kinsale the defeated Spanish Commander Don Juan Del'Aquila, lived here for some months before being repatriated to Spain. He was, by all accounts a wonderful success, socially, and was entertained regally by the gentry of the city for the duration of his stay. Unfortunately, for him, his return to Spain was not quite such a happy event and he was executed by his monarch because of the failure of the expedition. All these old laneways have been permitted to fall into decay. This is a great pity since they are the oldest districts, and, properly maintained, they could be a distinctive and attractive part of the city.

Close to the North Gate Bridge, Skiddy's Castle, the stronghold of that old Danish family (sometimes known as Scudamore) is commemorated by a plaque on the original site. Across the road, high up on the front wall of the building now occupied by Daly's wine merchants, there is a stone fireplace, reputed to have come from this castle.

'The Marsh' is that part of the city, west of the North Main Street and stretching from Washington Street north to the river. When the city began to be developed beyond the walls in the eighteenth century, all the marsh lands in this district were reclaimed, and the wealthy merchants began to build their homes in this area. One of the loveliest sites was

Bachelors Quay, on the south bank of the north channel. These old mansions contained some beautiful frescoes, particularly those by the Francini brothers, and while many of them have been destroyed some still remain. All these houses were sold, and over the years they degenerated into tenements until they were eventually razed by the corporation during their slum clearance schemes. One of the tragedies was the demolition of the Sherriff's house, at the west junction of Bachelors Quay and Grattan Street. The Sherriff's house was familiarly known as the 'Doll's House' and was a beautifully symmetrical structure. A scaled-down version of the 'Doll's House' is situated across the road from the School of Art in Emmet Place. The 'Doll's House' was featured in Frank O'Connor's, *The Saint and Mary Kate* and Donal Giltinan's, *Goldfish in the Sun.*

On the north bank of the river there stands the few remains of the Franciscan Friary 'Our Lady's Well'. The well still exists, as do some caves, said to be part of the old Abbey. It is said that Perkin Warbeck also stayed here during his sojourn in the city. After the Reformation the abbey was suppressed but despite the Penal Laws the friars continued to minister in the city. It appears that the Penal Laws were not rigidly enforced and in 1609 a house of the Order was again opened in the city. About this time also a set of beautiful chalices were presented to the community and these are still preserved in the House at Liberty Street. They had a centre in Cross Street and later in Broad Lane, and even though this site was abandoned in favour of the Liberty Street situation, almost two hundred years ago the church is still known as Broad Lane. The present church and monastery were built in the 1950s and while there are some interesting mosaic works, executed by Italian artists, the church itself is little more than a Byzantine barn. It is incongruous that in the middle of the twentieth century such a building – in complete contrast to whatever there is of a native school of architecture and divorced from all the trends of modern architecture – should have been constructed. It is disconcerting that most of the best architectural features of the city should be buildings commissioned by the non-Catholic religious denominations. There is a story of a parish priest who was instructing an architect on a commission which he was about to undertake: 'And mind you I don't want any of your foreign designs or anything like that. A nice bit of Gothic or Byzantine will do me fine.'

The Mansion House, residence of the Mayor, was designed by Davies Ducart in 1767. Nothing of importance appears to have taken place in this fine building, with its magnificent staircase, except that it was the starting point of the tri-annual pilgrimage of Throwing the Dart. Every third year the Mayor and his entourage journeyed from here to the harbour entrance and cermonially cast a dart into the sea, thereby denoting the extent of his jurisdiction. This building was subsequently purchased by the Sisters of Mercy and is now part of their hospital. It is situated at the corner of Henry Street. Across the road is the Malt House, considered to be an outstanding example of industrial architecture. This too has changed ownership and is now part of the University.

The Medical Dispensary in Grattan Street was formerly the Meeting House of the Society of Friends. The Quakers are now few in number in the city, only a few families remaining, but they enjoy a high reputation – during the Famine of the 1840s they donated £200,000 for relief work. The Society was introduced to Cork by two English members, Elizabeth Fletcher and Elizabeth Smith, about the year 1650. The first Meeting House was erected on this site in 1677 but was taken down and re-built in 1777. The present building was erected in 1833, to the design of G.T. Beale. Their burial ground is in Summerhill South. Like the Catholics, the nonconformist Quakers were frequently persecuted and on many occasions interned.

One of the earliest and certainly most celebrated members was William Penn. His family were in the possession of estates in Dundanion Castle, Blackrock, Ibaune, Imokilly, and Barryroe. While in England William Penn had become interested in the Society but his father disapproved and sent him to Ireland to remove him from their influence. Penn, however, renewed acquaintence with one of his English

72

friends in Ireland and was eventually received into the Society at their meeting house in Cork. At this time the Quakers were being persecuted by the City Mayor, of whom Penn was to say: 'Religion, which is at once my crime and mine innocence makes me a prisoner of a Mayor's malice.' Penn strove continuously to alleviate the position of the Quakers, travelling frequently to Dublin to plead their case, and it was during this period, when the Quakers visited an imprisoned member and were then themselves imprisoned by the gaoler, that the tradition of 'meetings' is said to have originated. Penn himself was eventually arrested and lodged in the Tower of London, but his father contrived to have him released. Subsequently he sailed to America and founded the State of Pennsylvania. The Quakers survived these prosecutions; many more came after Cromwell and eventually prospered, being among the most respected merchants in the city. At times, indeed, the City Fathers were compelled to borrow money from them to maintain the city finances. It was another Quaker, Edward Martyn who, conscious and concerned at the appalling poverty obtaining in the city, and convinced that the cause of it was drink, approached Father Mathew and suggested a crusade against drink. The Capuchin priest, a brilliant orator and organizer, poured his energies into the effort and had enormous success. An indication of this success may be gathered from the following figures;

	1839	1842
Sale of liquor	12,296,000 gals	6,485,443 gals
Duty	£1,434,573	£864,725
Prisoners	12,049	9,875

Father Mathew, who was a member of a family involved in distilleries, inaugurated the movement by signing the pledge at a public meeting in Patrick Street. There is a rather indifferent statue, by Foley, in memory of Father Theobald Mathew in Patrick Street. Locals wits say of it, that Father Mathew with his right hand stretching palm downwards is saying, 'Era, shure I've been drinking myself since I was that high.'

Liberty Street which connects Grattan Street to the Main Street was up to this century the milk market for the city. Every day the farmers brought their churns of milk into the city and the housekeepers thronged into Liberty Street to purchase their daily supplies. Apparently the advantage was that the farmers were inclined to be a bit more generous with their measure and the extra measure was called a 'tilly'.

The Courthouse was constructed in 1835 to the design of the Pain Brothers. On Good Friday 1891, it suffered severe damage in a fire and in the subsequent reconstruction only the original front wall and portico were retained. The design of the new building was by William H. Hill and the builder was Samuel Hill. One of the most striking features of the new building was the Copula, which was supported by marble pillars. The marble used was black Kilkenny, green Connemara, red Cork, and dove Meath. The Courtrooms differed from those in the old building in that they were rectangular in shape whereas the old ones had been circular. In addition, there were witness boxes. In the old days the witnesses sat on a chair which was placed on top of a desk, under the judge's bench. The fire of 1891 was a serious blow to the city archives as many of the irreplaceable documents were destroyed. This new building which was opened in 1895 replaced a series of older buildings. In addition to the premises now occupied by Brown Thomas in the Grand Parade, there were court-houses in Paradise Place, and the Court of Conscience and the magistrates court in Cornmarket Street.

At the point where Castle Street meets the Grand Parade there is the renowned Coal Quay. The correct name for this street is Cornmarket Street, the Coal Quay itself being on the quayside. This open air market has been known since its inception as the Coal Quay. It now has only a shadow of its former importance, but for many Cork people it is the essence of the city. Up to recent years it was the principal market for the city, the market gardeners bringing in their produce every morning but especially on Tuesdays, Thursdays, and Saturdays. It was so busy that the carts spilled out of the street and down Lavitt's Quay as far as the Opera House. Business began at six o'clock in the morning and to cater for the early arrivals the bars in the locality enjoyed the privilege of early opening at seven o'clock. There were many restaurants in the street, among the best known being Maggie Murphy's, Kearney's, and Mother Regan's, and a local balladeer sang their praises –

'There's a restaurant called Kearney's don't you see
Where you'll get a feather bed/and a fine feed of pig's head
But don't forget to pay before you leave.'

In addition to the farmers, shopkeepers and eating-house proprietors, the local jobbers made their living in the market. The potato market also provided another family with a living. Originally the Tobins and later the Flynns hired their weighing machines to the farmers charging a fee of two pence a bag for weighing the potatoes and they also provided a storage for unsold goods. The Coal Quay was more or less a family affair, the stalls being handed down from one generation to another. Renowned in its day for the effervescence of the repartee and the loyalty of the stall holders to each other against outside interests, it has for practical purposes succumbed to so-called progress, the dreadful rush to uniformity and 'respectability'. The Bazar Market on Cornmarket has a very pleasant cut-stone front with a central bay, while underneath are four half columns and a well proportioned cornice running the whole length. There are two beautifully carved coats of arms in high relief at each end above the cornice. Much of this enclosed market has been leased and is now used as a wholesale supermarket. What remains, still operates as a second-hand clothes and junk market but, as the leases expire, they are not being reissued. In addition the supermarket group have offered to buy the rights of the remaining stalls as they plan to extend their business. It will mean the end of the 'Coal Quay'.

Paul Street is the narrow thoroughfare running parallel to

Patrick Street and at the side of St Peter and Paul's Church. St Peter and Paul's School has been described by Seamus Murphy as 'a garden in stone'. They are all there, primrose, lilies, fern, roses, marigolds, apples, thistles, shamrocks buttercups, geranium, and vine. Paul's Lane is a narrow laneway close by the school. Many years ago, late at night, a gentleman strolling along spied 'a lady in white' moving along the laneway. Convinced that it was an apparition of the Virgin he reported the occurence to the parish priest who immediately began investigations. He soon discovered the presence of a brothel in Paul's Lane and it transpired that the 'virgin' was one of the ladies, clad in a night dress, escaping from the clutches of a too ardent client!

The church of St Peter and Paul is one of the city's architectural pleasures and one whose history is of great interest. It stands on the site of the old Carey's Lane Church which was completed in 1786. The present church, in the Neo-gothic style, was designed by the younger Pugin and the builder was Mr Barry McMullen. It was opened for services 29 June 1866 and consecrated by Bishop Delaney. The altar was designed by Mr G.C. Ashley and built in the workshops of Mr Samuel Daly in Cook Street and consecrated 10 August 1874. Although the church was never completed according to the original drawings, it is yet a wonderful example of this style. It contains some wonderful stone and wood carvings, done by Hogan himself. On an occasion when a priest was escorting a group of visitors round the church, one asked him if perhaps the carvings had been executed by a local artist. The priest insisted that no local man was capable of creating such workmanship. Then a gentleman, overhearing the remark, drew the priest's attention to one of the angel figures on which was inscribed 'Executed by John Hogan of Cork', and then he added, 'Father, I'm John Hogan!'

The church was commissioned by Father John Murphy, a member of a wealthy Cork family of brewers. In his youth John Murphy left his native city and for a time lived in London. He was not a success in business and decided to try his luck in the far off lands. He later spent some time in

China before returning to London. He then decided to try his luck in the 'colonies' and left for Canada where he joined the Hudson Bay Company. He served with this mammoth organization before suddenly leaving and joining up with a group of Red Indians with whom he lived for about six years. It was during this time that he earned himself the name 'Black Eagle'. Having met a group of friars in the wilderness, he was apparantly very much impressed because he returned home to Cork and subsequently entered a novitiate and began to study for the priesthood. Ordained, he served for many years in Liverpool before being recalled to Cork and appointed to the Parish of SS Peter and Paul, in the heart of the city, as the new Parish Priest. It was during his ministry that the church was commissioned and built. As has been already noted, the church has never been completed and the great western window was added at late as 1935.

The Crawford Municipal School of Art in Emmet Place has a history going back as far as 1724. The northern wing was then erected but as a Customs House. In 1832 it was handed over to the Royal Cork Institution, a body founded in 1807, with the object of 'diffusing knowledge and the application of science to the common purposes of life'. In 1850 a group of prominent Cork citizens approached the English Government for a grant to establishment of a school of design, and they were successful in their efforts. In 1884 it became necessary to extend the building. Mr Sharman Crawford, a member of the brewing family, agreed to defray the cost of the extension of the building. The extension is the work of Mr A. Hill, who succeeded brilliantly in blending the addition with the Old Custom House into a harmonious whole. The Gallery was officially opened by the Prince of Wales.

The School of Art contains a comprehensive display of works of art with particular reference to Ireland. Among the artists whose work is on display are Sean Keating, Sir William Orpen, Jack B. Yeats, Sean O'Sullivan, Seamus Murphy, Nathaniel Hone, Paul Henry, Sir John Lavery, Robert Gibbings, etc, etc.

The collection in the Gallery has been supplemented over

the years by several bequests, including the Gibson and Barrett Bequest, the Chester Beatty Loan Collection, and numerous individual gifts and loans. Another body which had been operating successfully for the advancement of painting and sculpture was the Royal Society for the Promotion of Fine Arts, founded in 1815. Its Patrons were the Prince Regent, later George IV, and the Lord Lieutenant.

In 1818 Pope Pius VII – in appreciation of the services rendered by the English Government in arranging the return to Italy of works of art confiscated by Napoleon – presented the Prince with a collection of plaster casts, taken from the originals in the Vatican Museum. The plaster casts were especially executed by Canova. Through the efforts of Lord Ennismore, this collection was presented to the Royal Cork Society. Later when this society amalgamated with the Royal Cork Institution the collection was presented to the Crawford Municipal School of Art. An unusual item in the possession of the Gallery is an embroidered bedspread, designed and made for the Emperor Charles V in the sixteenth century. The Crawford Municipal School of Art, in addition to its function as an art gallery has also functioned as a teaching institution. Probably its most famous pupils were the great Daniel Maclise and Samuel Forde.

The Central Hall, Academy Street is the social centre of the Methodist Church in Cork. Methodism was introduced to Cork very early in its history by two of John Wesley's own assistants. The earliest meetings were conducted in the open air, probably on the green where Sheares' and Henry Streets are now situated. Wesley himself paid many visits to the city – the last in 1789 – and preferred to speak in the open air, this site being a particular favourite of his. In 1752 he suggested a meeting house be erected and subsequently a tract of land was purchased and a church erected in Henry Street. The first Sunday School in Ireland was opened adjacent to the church and continued in operation until the hall in Academy Street was opened. For a short time the Methodists met in the Huguenot Church in French Church Street but on Sunday 7 April 1805 the new Wesley Church was open-

ed in Patrick's Street at a cost of £2,272. Repairs and renovations were executed in 1855 and yet again in 1872. The
Academy Hall was opened in March 1889. It was then decided
to erect a new church and in 1895 the Barrackton Church was
completed.

French Church Street is named after the church of the
Huguenots which stood in this street. The Huguenots camè
to Ireland after the St Bartholomew's Day Massacre in
France. It was somewhat ironic that they should seek sanctuary in a country which even then was suffering religious
persecution of its own. The Huguenots brought with them
considerable industrial skills. They revitalized the arts of
glass making and introduced silk manufacture. Their church
was eventually closed and sold, and until it was destroyed
by fire in recent years it was a warehouse. Their graveyard
was alongside the church and, although it has been concret-
ed over, some of the old headstones are preserved.

In 1955 a disastrous fire razed the Cork Opera House. It
was one of the worst disasters that could have possibly hit
the city, breaking a continuity of cultural activities which
had enriched the city for generations. Over the years the
Opera House had created for itself a wonderful tradition,
integrating into its activities all the various classes in the
city. It had been host to such a varied programme – from
ballet to boxing, from opera to Gilbert and Sullivan – that
it had effectively brought the people to appreciate its value.

In the old days when touring companies visited the city,
among them the opera groups, Moody Manners, Carl Rosa,
and the Meara Opera Co. would arrive at the railway station be greeted by the populace, the horses taken out of the
shafts, and the carriages hauled through the streets to their
digs. The artists stayed in lodgings close to the Opera
House, at Lavitts Quay, and Sean O'Faolain remembered
their staying at his home in Half Moon Street. The 'Gods'
or upper balcony, had the reputation of being a very critical
audience, reserving the privilege of showing their displea-
sure as well as their acclaim. In time it came to be said that
if a company could pass an Opera House audience they
could pass any audience. There must be a grain of truth in

the tradition of the dockers with the coal dust still on their faces and the opera score on their knees closely following the score and correcting when necessary the mistakes of the artists. Certainly there is no doubt that many of the various associations in the city, the Ancient Order of Hibernians, the Catholic Young Men's Society, and others generally visited the Opera House in groups. During the intervals members would entertain the audience with their rendition of popular numbers, and the custom arose of the curtains not being drawn after the interval until the singer had finished in the 'Gods'. There is a well authenticated story of the occasion when the tenor in stage failed to hit a high note and a gentleman in the 'Gods' obliged. At the end of the performance the tenor, on being presented on stage, duly thanked the gentleman for his help.

The audience were never slow to voice their disapproval of a performance, and at times these protests took on the intensity of a riot – as was the case when *The Royal Divorce* was performed, bottles and other missiles were hurled at the performers and a riot did in fact develop.

The theatrical season attracted the annual visits of companies such as the Carl Clopet, Ilsey McCabe, and many others. It was quite usual for these companies to supplement the cast with local actors to play bit parts. On one occasion when Stanley Ilsey and Leo McCabe were playing Somerset Maugham's *Rain* two men from the parish where hired to play the parts of natives. On the Friday night their friends and neighbours packed the front two rows of the balcony and whenever the 'natives' appeared on stage the slagging from the 'Gods' was terrific. One of the men was the medico for the local football team, a position which had earned for him the nickname 'The Doc'. At the end of the performance when actors were taking their bows the cry came down from the 'Gods' 'We want the Doc!'

The doctor in the cast, no doubt impressed, made several appearances only to be met with the chant 'Not you, we want The Doc'. Needless to say the real 'Doc' kept his mouth shut and remained off stage! Over the years the reputation of the Opera House was so great that it became a habit for people to pay a weekly visit to the theatre and this contributed to a wonderful appreciation of the arts in the city. It must be admitted, however, that the bar in the 'Gods', the Round Bar, under the roof, had the reputation of serving the worst pint of stout in the city.

After the burning of the Opera House in 1955 there was a lapse of many years while the various groups argued backwards and forwards as to the shape and capacity of the new Opera House. Although the smaller theatres rallied round to try and fill the gap left by the loss of the old building the effect on the theatre in Cork was profound. The tradition of the weekly visit to the Opera House was all but lost. When eventually the design for the new Opera House was announced it created a fresh storm of criticism. The plans provided for a theatre of 1,000 seating capacity. The theatre lobby advocated a smaller capacity more suitable for plays; they pointed out that the Irish tradition was in this field; that a large theatre would be very difficult to fill over a run of several weeks; that the overheads would be excessive. The members of the operatic and musical fraternities demonstrated that a small theatre would be unsuitable for musicals and similar stage shows. In addition to all this the Opera House – while obtaining substantial grants from the State and the Corporation and a tremendous response from local people – was a private company and as such concerned with the financial aspect of things. Eventually it was decided to build the 1,000 seat theatre. Only time and experience will prove, if it hasn't already done so, the wisdom of this decision.

CHAPTER 9

The commercial and social centre of the city is circumscribed by Patrick's Street, the Grand Parade, the South
Mall, and Parnell Place. It is an area which lay outside the
old walled city, on a district called Dunscombes Marsh. The
reclamation and building of this area began in the seventeenth century, gathered speed in the eighteenth and was
completed in the nineteenth century. The work necessitated
the arching over of many of the streams which flowed between the various islands and the construction of bridges.
There was a drawbridge near the site of the present Drawbridge Street; a bridge stretching from Daunts Square to the
junction of Patrick's Street and the Grand Parade; and another from Tuckey Street to Oliver Plunkett Street, Castle
Street, Patrick Street, the Grand Parade, Tuckey Street,
and the South Mall were among the river courses which
were reclaimed. The marshy nature of the soil posed many
problems for the builders. As recently as the construction of
the Bank of Ireland in the South Mall, a pile of concrete
blocks about 10 feet high slowly subsided into the ground
and when the Electricity Supply Board Offices were
being constructed a concrete pile driven into the founda-
tions disappeared overnight.

Patrick's Street is the primary shopping area, and the
complex of streets around Oliver Plunkett Street is a very
important, if secondary, area. The banking, insurance and
legal businesses are located in the South Mall. All the principal hotels and restaurants are located here; the theatres and
cinemas are also within this area.

The reclamation of Patrick's Street or 'Pana' as it is
known has been proceeding for a long time and a corporation minute of the 1830s recommended the demolition of
the drawbridge, it being noted that 'most of the street was
then vaulted over'. Before the advent of the cinema and tel-

evision, the principal recreation of the people was 'doing Pana' a form of Celtic Paseo, walking up and down Patrick's Street meeting friends and acquaintances. The street, following the line of the water course, curves around in a wonderful horseshoe shape, distinguished by many fine limestone buildings. Many of its most imposing buildings are of comparatively recent construction. In 1920 the notorious Black and Tans, – as a reprisal for an ambush, – ran amok in the city and proceeded to set fire to the city centre as well as the City Hall. The extent of the destruction is quite apparent if one studies the different styles of architecture of the street. The fine buildings stretching from Roches Stores to the Victoria were those rebuilt by the British Government as compensation for the attack.

The buildings flanking Patrick's Street still retain a peculiar connection with the days before the reclamation of the thoroughfare. The head lease of each house contains a covenant granting the owners mooring rights to the river. The only physical reminder of those days is the flight of steps over the entrance to the 'Le Chateau' bar, opposite the Victoria Hotel. The offices of the *Cork Examiner* were formerly a theatre.

The premises now occupied by Guy and Co. at 70, Patrick's Street were at the turn of the nineteenth century occupied by a Mr Bolster. This gentleman was a member of the artistic and literary movement in the city. He published a magazine in which he encouraged young poets. It appears that he was a little dilatory in making payments and earned for himself the uncomplimentary title of 'The Cork screw'. He was one of the first to appreciate the talents of Daniel Maclise. When Sir Walter Scott was visiting the city he arranged to call to Mr Bolster's Shop. Bolster, in turn, arranged that Maclise should be present; hidden, it is said, behind a curtain. While Scott was engaged in his business Maclise did a quick sketch of the author and then returned to his home in Sheares Street to complete the portrait. Bolster later hung it in his window, and when Scott returned for his purchases he was shown the work. Impressed, he autographed it. The approval of Scott added much to the reputation of Maclise who later opened a studio in Patrick's Street. His fee for a commission was thirty shillings. Maclise illustrated the first edition of Moore's melodies, and was sent to London, where he became one of the foremost portrait painters of his day.

The craft of gold and silver smithing in Cork is an old and very reputable one, old and modern Cork silver possesses a very high reputation. One of the oldest surviving firms in Cork is that of Egans of Patrick's Street. This firm was founded by Mr William Egan who was apprenticed to the trade of silversmith about 1820. In the first half of the nineteenth century there were apparently about fifty craftsmen engaged in the trade but by 1850 the numbers had been greatly reduced and Egans were possibly the only firm to survive. In 1883, Mr Clare the foreman jeweller at Egans, designed and executed the famous model of Shandon Church and Steeple which was first shown at the Exhibition of 1883. Subsequently it was shown at exhibitions all over the world. In 1910 Egans decided to expand their business and immediately brought workmen from Dublin and the necessary equipment was purchased. From the beginning the late Mr Barry Egan determined that it should be truly Cork Silver and steps were taken to train apprentices. In 1911 the firm was commissioned by the President of University college Cork Sir Bertram Windly, to design the College mace and this work was executed in the various departments of the firm. The mace in solid silver is decorated with jewels and enamel ware and is a beautiful piece of workmanship. The firm also executed the Coronation Cup in solid silver, presented by King George V to the Cork City Race committee.

The Civil War situation, in 1922, created a peculiar problem for Egans. Cork and practically all of Munster was in control of the Republicans while the remainder of the country was in the hands of the Free State Forces. At the time, Egans had almost one thousand ounces of silver ready to be sent to Dublin to be hall-marked. However, communications and transport being in such a precarious position, Mr Barry Egan was very loath to send his hand-wrought silver to

Dublin. He decided to continue to make silver, assaying and stamping the pieces himself with two dies designed by himself and his engraver. These dies resemble the old Cork marks in that they consist of a castle and a ship, but the new Republican ship differs from the old ship in that it has two masts only, whereas the original Cork ship is three masted. Egans stamped all the silver produced between the months, July-September 1922 with this mark, and so Cork Republican Silver came into being. When peace was eventually restored, silver was again sent to Dublin to be hall-marked. The pieces of Republican Silver are of course illegal and no dealer could openly sell it. In all there were some sixty pieces and Mr Barry Egan acquired this privately from the firm and subsequently disposed of about forty pieces which are now considerable value not only because of their historical connotations but also on account of their intrinsic worth. The material is of standard assay, hand wrought, hammered between hammer and anvil, and not soft machine-made silver. The dies used have of course been destroyed.

The Victoria Hotel we find mentioned in Joyce's *Portrait of the Artist as a Young Man* but then, of course, his father was a Corkman. It was in the Victoria hotel that Parnell stayed the night before the election in which he headed the poll in Cork. And what a marvellous opening statement he made that night: 'Citizens of Cork, this is the night before the battle. To your guns then!' And it was also in Cork, on 21 January 1885, that he spoke the words now inscribed on his monument in O'Connell Street Dublin,

'...but no man has a right to fix the boundary of the march of a nation. No man has a right to say "Thus far shalt thou go, and no further"; and we have never attempted to fix the NE PLUS ULTRA to the progress of Ireland's nationhood, and we never shall...'

The Irish tend to idolize their revolutionaries and to forget or minimize their parliamentarians. Before the crushing anguish of the Kitty O'Shea divorce, Charles Stewart Parnell was the 'uncrowned king' of Ireland. He is remembered in Cork by a bridge and an unimposing street called after him.

Up to recently his supporters, once a year, wore an ivy leaf in his memory. Even after the tragedy of the divorce action, there was still a chance that Parnell would rally the Irish Parliamentary Party around him and at that fateful meeting, in room 16 of the Houses of Parliament, when the die was finally cast, he almost succeeded. Tim Healy stood between him and the impossible. The Parnellite faction were actually carrying the day and Parnell sensing the swing of the meeting to him arose, and demanding that he get order, commanded: 'Order, order, remember I am still the master of this party!' Healy was on his feet in a flash with one of the most devastating replies of all time 'Yes, and we know who the mistress is too!' It was the end of Parnell and soon he was to die, still a comparatively young man, in England.

Churchill was to say that Tim Healy was the greatest orator he had ever heard in Parliament. He was the master of repartee, swift, savage, and preemptive. On one particular occasion Healy had made a most bitter attack on a deceased member of the House, concluding with the statement 'Gentlemen he has joined Cromwell'. There was uproar in the house, members demanding that Healy should withdraw the remark. He waited until order was restored and then commented: 'Gentlemen it appears to me that you all know where poor old Cromwell is.'

H.V. Morton in his book *In Search of Ireland* commented that it was impossible for an Englishman to follow an Irish argument; that the Irish state the major premise, jump to the conclusion and then argue the ins and outs of the case; that analogies are freely discussed and humour is an integral part of the argument. Of Corkmen he added that they stay up half the night conceiving aphorisms to amuse their friends the following night. It may be that the introduction of the mass media of communication and the discouragement of heckling at political meetings have contributed, but the art of oratory in Ireland is a shadow of its former self. One of its last great exponents, now retired from the scene, was James Dillon. During a debate in the Dail the Minister for Justice was asked the number of police who attended 'Le Petit Ball', a function attended by the 'aristocracy' of Europe at the beautiful Powerscourt House. The Minister replied that 106 policemen and two police women had been on duty. James Dillon's voice was heard: 'Minister, was that a dance or an insurrection?' Mr De Valera was once injudicious enough to question the contribution of James Dillon's ancestors to Irish public life. Dillon stormed to the defence. Yes, his father before him had been active in Irish politics, and where were Mr De Valera's? 'Banging banjoes in Barcelona!'

One of the most extraordinary and least known figures in Irish life, the socialist William Thompson, lived in Patrick's Street. The old saying that a prophet is never recognized in his own country was never truer than in the case of William Thompson, regarded in others as one of the truly original thinkers of the nineteenth century. Karl Marx found inspiration in the writings of Thompson but in his mighty *Das Kapital* concedes only one rather begrudging reference. Thompson was born in Rosscarbery about 1785. He was a wealthy and, strange to say, a benevolent landlord. He was one of the first to conceive of the idea of Co-operatives and proceeded to establish one at Carhoogarriffe, near Skibbereen, County Cork. Unfortunately he died before he could guide it to success, although he had already recruited a group of people to participate and had built a housing scheme. Even in death Thompson was controversial and his will was contested, and after a lengthy legal battle which ate up most of the fortune the will was declared invalid on the grounds of immorality! It appears that Thompson had reservations about the concept of matrimony and the constitution of the co-operative had stipulated that the members should live a truly co-operative existence without the benefit of marriage.

William Thompson was buried with full Christian ceremonial but a reading of the will expressly stated that his wish was that he should be interred without the benefit of Christian, Mohammedan, or Hindu rites. Soon after a French phrenologist sought and was granted permission to exhume the body and remove the skull that he might study the cranium of this extraordinary Corkman. The writings of

Thompson are only now beginning to attract the attention of Irish politicians and scholars and a cause of much regret is that it is thought that three further manuscripts were destroyed by the family on his death.

The Grand Parade is called, in Irish, the Street of the Yellow Horse. An equestrian statue stood at the river end of the street. The statue had a rather unfortunate history, the head of the British monarch having been thrice changed to cater for the shift of political opinion in England. It then transpired that the horse could not stand on its two rear legs and a prop had to be inserted to keep the statue upright. In 1867 the statue mysteriously disappeared: in all probability dumped into the nearby river.

The building now occupied by the Queen's Old Castle at the other end of the Grand Parade has an interesting history. It stands on the side of the Kings Castle, the Queen's Castle being originally on the position of Daunt's Square. These are the two castles represented on the coat of arms of the city and demonstrate quite clearly the extent of the old walled city. This building was originally the courthouse. When constructed, it was declared a separate authority so that rates and other charges would not be paid to the corporation. One of the most famous trials conducted in this building was the celebrated case 'The Doneraile Conspiracy'. A group of men from the vicinity of Doneraile, County Cork were arrested and charged with being members of the Whiteboys, an organization engaged in the land agitation movement. The men were innocent, but the authorities were determined to make an example of them. Daniel O'Connell was chosen as the defence lawyer. O'Connell made a spectacular non-stop ride from his home in Derrynane, County Kerry, to arrive in time and with a brilliant defence succeeded in saving the case. His reputation as a defence lawyer was supreme and he boasted that he could drive a coach and four through any English law. In contrast to the Sheares Brothers who had been very impressed by the French Revolution, O'Connell was completely prejudiced against it by the unrest and executions and abhorred violence. Having killed a man in a duel he always wore a black glove in his hand.

He was the first Catholic to be elected to the British Parliament and then challenged and overcame the provision excluding Catholics from taking their seats.

After the successful campaign of Catholic Emancipation he turned his attention to the national front and let the movement for the repeal of the Act of Union and the establishment of Home Rule for Ireland. His leadership of the Irish people was unquestioned and Sean O'Faolain has called him *King of the Beggars*. The threat posed by O'Connell reached such proportions that the authorities proscribed one of a series of monster meetings organized by him. Influenced by his abhorrence of violence and intimidated when the authorities sent a gunboat up the Liffey, O'Connell relented and cancelled the meeting at Clontarf. As it had been for the Danes in 1014, Contarf was O'Connell's Waterloo. His control of the movement vanished almost overnight and soon he was to die in Italy. In his will he asked 'his soul to heaven, his heart to Rome and his body to Ireland'.

His anitpathy to revolution and violence has not endeared O'Connell to the Irish Republicans, his opposition to Davis and the Young Irelanders has neither been forgotten nor forgiven; and his much quoted phrase that 'the freedom of Ireland was not worth the shedding of one drop of blood' is about as contentious a statement as anyone could make. He himself was a native speaker of the Irish Language, but he denied it its place in the life of the people, speaking only English at the great rallies even though most of the people did not understand him. More than any other individual he contributed to the decline in the fortunes of the Language. Nor was he pre-eminent as a social thinker – in Parliament he opposed a Bill outlawing the employement of children under eight years of age in the mines. The stained-glass window behind the High altar in The Holy Trinity Church is in his memory.

The South Mall is the centre of the banking, legal and insurance business in Cork. It is said that more wealth is accumulated in this street than in any other comparable one in Europe – a good example of local pride but inaccurate.

The history of banking in Cork goes back to 1675 when Edward and Joseph Hoare opened the first bank outside of Dublin in Cork. It was immediately successful, and Edward Hoare was in time elected Alderman, Sheriff, and Mayor of Cork. The Hoares married into the prominent banking families of Pikes, Gurnell's and Gurneys, and a Hoare was associated with the firm of Barrett, Hoare and Co. Ltd., now absorbed in Lloyd's Bank. One of the Hoares married a member of the Pike family whose bank was wound up in 1825, all the creditors being paid in full. It was one of the few banks which survived the financial crisis of 1820.

The firm of Roger Travers and Sheares which subsequently became known as Sheares Bank and which was founded in the middle of the eighteenth century closed on the death of Mr Sheares at the turn of the nineteenth century. The brothers Sheares, members of the United Ireshmen and executed for their participation in that organization, were of this family.

Daniel Maclise, the great artist, worked as a clerk in the firm of Newenhams Bank which closed in 1825, again all the creditors being paid in full. The bankers, Morris Leycester and McCall formed the nucleus of the Bank of Ireland, opened a branch in Cork in 1826 with Mr Leycester as agent.

All these were private banks but the picture changed radically with the concept of the joint stock company. The Provincial Bank of Ireland opened in 1825. It drew much of its support from the milling industry in the early days. The Hibernian Bank was introduced to Cork in 1866 and the National Bank of Ireland was closely associated with the financing of the Cork Butter Market.

The Munster and Leinster Bank was founded in 1885 with local support and the idea of helping the farming community. Charles Stewart Parnell wrote commending it to the public. The Head Office, in the South Mall, was designed by Mr Hill and constructed by John Sisk and Son Ltd. The dome is supported by eight marble pillars. Six of these pillars were originally intended for the organ loft of the Old St Pauls of London but were not used and Mr Hill acquired them for this building. It then became necessary to obtain a further two pillars but inquiries revealed that the quarries at Spezia, Italy had been closed for a hundred years. Eventually arrangements were made to have the quarries re-opened and the two additional pillars were duly cut and dispatched to Cork.

A reasonable well-authenticated story has it that a Corkman, on a pilgrimage to Rome, visited the Sistine Chapel. The official guide asked him what he thought of the building 'Era, 'tis alright, but you should see the Munster and Leinster Bank in Cork!'

Local pride knows no bounds, and it is well exemplified in the story. Christy Ring, probably the greatest hurler of all time, was granted a personal audience by the Pope. A photograph duly appeared on the local paper. A Blackpool man looked at it and commented, 'Hey, who's the fellow there with Ringy?'

Before the South Mall was arched over in 1801, much of the trade associated with the provisioning of the British Army, engaged in the Continental Wars, was conducted through the Port of Cork. During the Napoleonic Wars Cork shipped so much cured beef that it was recognized as the second port in the country. The ships, rather than return empty and face a rough passage, brought bricks from Holland as ballast. These bricks were used in the construction of buildings. An outstanding example is the yellow brick building adjoining the Imperial Hotel, while another is the pair of houses now known as Trinity House on George's Quay. In a similar manner, the ships bringing coal from Newcastle took on stone from the Little Island Quarry and some of the municipal buildings in that city are constructed of Little Island limestone.

The Commercial Buildings Co. was incorporated by Royal Charter in 1808. The main object of the association was to provide a suitable building where members could meet to conduct their business. The members agreed to subscribe £100 each to defray the cost of the building and in 1811, Sir Thomas Deane was commissioned to design a building at a cost of £7,000. It was completed in 1813. This is the building now forming part of the Imperial Hotel in the South Mall. The facilities included a coffee house and restaurant and sleeping accommodation for a small number of people. The total cost of the building was £10,000.

In 1813 the company petitioned Parliament and was granted permission to introduce the 'Commercial Buildings Act' of 1814. The act provided for the imposition of a special duty of 'one shilling British on all entries, inwards and outwards in the port of Cork (post entries only excepted), to be collected by the Collector of that Port and paid to the Treasurer of your petitioners, said Company. One half whereof to be by said Company applied towards completing and maintaining said Commercial Buildings, and the other half towards improving the Quays, Canals, and River of Cork.'

In 1816, the company again commissioned Sir Thomas Deane to design a 'hotel and tavern' behind the Commercial Buildings in Pembroke Street. This was the Imperial Hotel and was completed in 1819. In the same year it was let to a Mr Joyce for a term of five years at a rental of £700 P.A.

The Cork and County Club is the last bastion of British Imperialism in Ireland – in the 'Republic' that is – and during the 'troubles' was the scene of one of the most famous executions of those times. The infamous Major Smith, in a fit of fury after a successful ambush by the I.R.A. ordered the Royal Irish Constabularly 'to shoot on sight'. To their credit, many members of that body resigned in protest. To the discredit of the Kerry Brigades, Smith was permitted to leave the county is safety. Not that this ommission was unusual on the part of the Kerry Brigades, as during the Civil War, Michael Collins, horrified at the atrocities perpetrated there, commented that when they were most needed 'they ran into their black valleys where neither friend nor foe could find them'. Major Smith arrived in Cork and stayed in the County Club. One evening about nine o'clock a 'delegation' from the 'Boys' entered the club, asked to see Major Smith, and then approached him. Was he the man who had given the 'shoot on sight' command? Yes it was he. They drew their guns and shot him in the chair in which he was sitting. They then walked out of the building and joined the crowds coming out of the Assembly Rooms Cinema. They were never apprehended. The story is told of a very well-known politician's visit to the club. He was escorted by a friend, a rather hot-headed republican, and both were entertained with a tour of the building. When they came to the room, the guide pointed out the chair in which Major Smith was sitting when he was shot. The guide commented that 'This is the chair in which Major Smith was sitting when he was murdered'.

'What do you mean murdered?' interrupted the republican 'Exef...cuted!'

On the night of 11/12 December 1920 during curfew-hours the British forces in the city in a reprisal against an ambush ran amok and set fire to the City Hall, the Carnegie Free Library and the centre of the city. This act of vandalism was subsequently debated in the British House of Commons and the Secretary of State for Ireland, Hamer Greenwood explained that a spark from the City Hall, travelling across the South Mall, the Oliver Plunkett Street area had caused the burning of Cork! In due course compensation was granted, but the money was subsequently spent on the construction of a housing scheme. Eventually the foundation stone was laid on 9 July 1932 by Mr DeValera. The building was designed by Mr S. S. Kelly and construction was by John Sisk and Son. The stone is Little Island lime-stone. The Lord Mayor of the time was Mr F. J. Daly. The ceremonial trowel, in silver decorated with a Celtic motif and an ivory handle was created by Mr O'Connell, the silversmith. In addition to its ceremonial use it also had a functional value as it could be used as a fish slice and a helper.

CHAPTER 10

Cork Harbour shares with Sydney and Rio De Janeiro the reputation of being one of the finest natural harbours in the world. Almost land-locked, the Lower Harbours provide a safe anchorage in all weathers and such sufficient and extensive draught of deep water that the entire British Atlantic Fleet could anchor in safety.

The coat of arms of the city shows a ship sailing between two castles and nothing could be more expressive of the harbour's importance in the development of the city. Although the city owes its original impetus to the settlement of St Finnbarr who conceived his monastery as the abode of a recluse, it was the Danes who fortified the walled town on a complex of islands in the river. The mastery of the Danes lay in their mastery of the sea and their superior navigational skill; and they introduced into Cork an appreciation of trading unappreciated and unpractised until then.

All through its long history the association between city and port has been indivisable and it is conceivable that were it not for the port St Finnbarr's Monastic Settlement would be no more than a Clonmacnoise or a Glendalough, magnificent but isolated.

It is a beautiful harbour, from the entrance between Cork Head and Poer Head, past the towering splendour of St Colman's Cathedral, the wooded slopes of Currabinny, Passage, Glenbrook and Monkstown, up the wide expanse of Lough Mahon and the picturesque Blackrock Castle and into the city. Even the giant cranes of the Verolme Cork Dockyard, silhouetted black against the early morning summer sky, like the cadavers of prehistoric monsters looming over their prey, take on a spectral beauty.

Stan Laurel of the Laurel and Hardy comedy team was greeted on arrival in the harbour on board a trans-Atlantic liner by the carillion of bells of Cobh Cathedral, playing their signature tune. He later wrote of the occasion as one of the emotive experiences of his life.

The first yacht club in the world, The Royal Cork Yacht Club, was founded in 1720. On 4 April, 1838 the *Sirius* was the first steam ship to cross the Atlantic, east to west. It was captained by a Corkman, Captain Roberts, and on charter to another Corkman, Mr Beale. The *Sirius* made two further voyages before being transferred to the Channel trade and foundering in Ballycotton harbour in 1847. The main shaft was installed in the Templemichael Shovel Mills. The first iron steamer was built in Cork in 1845.

It is of course necessary to distinguish between the Lower harbour at Cobh and Passage and the upper harbour in the city. Up to the middle of the last century the lower harbour was by far the most important section, the low draught of water in the river channel precluding all but the smallest boats from entering the city. The lower harbour has been intimately associated with the history of the trans-Atlantic Liner trade since the first Cunarder, the steamer *Canada* called on 6 November 1859. In 1928 there were 354 liner-calls to the harbour, but the decline in this trade is evident and in 1969 only 36 calls were made.

And before the liner there were the great three- and four-masted sailing ships, which made Cork their port of call after their voyages around the 'Horn' from the west coast of America, India, and Australia. The average time for a journey was 115 days but the three masted clipper *The Falls of Garry* made a sailing from Portland, Oregon, in 85 days. When steam-made sailing ships obsolete many were purchased by the Finns and continued in business for many years. As recent as August 1937, the sailing ship *Moshulu* out of Wallaroo, Australia, unloaded 4520 tons of grain at Cork.

It is now difficult to appreciate the volume of traffic passing through the harbour in the last century. In 1814 a report in the *Southern Reporter* recounted that 'We lately saw a fleet of 300 vessels at Cobh, either for convoy or trading'. About 1830, Thackeray, writing of Cork noted that he saw forty ships berthed at the wharves up to St

Patrick's Bridge. Before the installation of radio in ships it was necessary for them to call to port to ascertain if orders were to be collected and these calls obviously added to the density of traffic. However, about the middle of the last century a staff member of the Cork Harbour Commisioners remembered a fleet of 365 ships in the harbour.

The Port contributed handsomely to the economy of the city, engaging a considerable labour force. There were the dockers, carters, employees of the harbour commisioners the Chanel Shipping Companies, importers of coal, timber, minerals, fertilizers and grain and the exporters of livestock, provisions etc. There was work for the stevedores, shipbrokers, and the employees of the dockyards.

It was inevitable that the volume of traffic would create the need for a repair service and this in turn would stimulate a shipbuilding industry. Before steam and iron the country abounded in suitable timber, and while the records are pitifully scarce and the general picture obscure it is certain that an industry functioned from earliest times. The first steamer built in Ireland, the appropriately named *City of Cork* was launched 13 June 1815 and plied the harbour traffic between Tuckey St Cork and Cobh, at a cost of sixpence a journey. Between 1845 and 1865, fifty-six vessels including sixteen one hundred ton barges were launched in the harbour. These vessels were up to 1350 tons net register and 270 feet in length. The widespread use of iron contributed to the decline of this industry but the recently founded Verolme Cork Dockyard is putting Cork back on the ship building scene.

A feature of the harbour traffic was the passenger lighters which travelled between the city and the lower harbour on scheduled services. The Citizens River Steamer Company had a fleet of four paddle boats which plied from St Patrick's Bridge to Cobh, Aghada, Currabinny and Crosshaven. The Passage Railway Company had three paddle boats, generally known as the 'green boats' plying between Passage, Glenbrook Pier, Monkstown Pier. Later, when the Passage Railway Company extended their service to Crosshaven the 'green boats' gradually went out of commission.

The city docks are somewhat unique in that, unlike most other ports, they are not enclosed and are accessible to the citizens, a consideration which has always been availed of fully and walking down the docks has always been a Sunday morning pastime. In the latter half of the last century and the beginning of the present century when the coastal trade was yet considerable the docks must have presented a fascinating scene. Ships came, literally, from all parts of the world and discharged some unusual cargoes. From Norway came ice, cut in four foot blocks from that country's frozen lakes and after being discharged at the quays it was stored in the city warehouses and in 'ice houses' such as are still in Lough Road and in other parts of the city. It was, and still is, somewhat ironic that a country which supplied the oak for the construction of the British Fleet, should eventually find it necessary to import timber. While much of it came from Canada, a considerable quantity came from Norway. The long beams, sometimes 80 feet in length and 2½ feet square presented a problem as they could be neither loaded nor unloaded in the normal manner. Special hatches or portholes were cut in the ships' bows, the beams were slid in and the portholes sealed for the voyage. On arrrival in port the hatches were opened and the timber unloaded into the river, the logs bound together to form huge rafts. The rafts were then floated up the river under St Patrick's bridge, up the Blackpool River to the timber yards in Letrim Street. It was this practice, probably, that gave the name Pouraddy Harbour to this part of Blackpool. Similarly rafts were floated up the South Channel to Harte's timber yard at Clarkes Bridge.

As in other ports a pilotage service is available to guide ships to their berths. While the early records of the service are unavailable it appears that before 1820 it was conducted on the basis of private enterprise, the pilots negotiating their own terms with the various shipping companies and agents. The Act of 1820 conferred on the Harbour Commissioners this function but the practise of private enterprise was continued until about 1890. Finally the Pilotage Act of 1913 clarified the position. It provided for the establishment of a

Pilot Fund, whereby all the fees were pooled and divided at the end of the year. This procedure is still followed and while the pilots are permitted an annual salary from the Harbour Commissioners, their remuneration is ultimately dependent on the collection of fees.

The early history of the port is obscure, possibly reflecting the relative unimportance of Cork as compared to Kinsale, Youghal, or Waterford. In 1500 Henry VII granted a charter under which the Mayor was given jurisdiction over the waters of the harbour extending from the city to a line drawn from Cork Head to Poer Head. Every three years escorted by the Council members he sailed out into the harbour and cast a dart into the sea thereby reasserting authority. This practice of throwing the Dart was continued until the early years of this century.

The motto included in the city coat of arms reads *Statio Bene Fida Carinis* and has been translated rather freely as follows;

A faithful friendly Cove
Where ships can safely ride
When Tempests, loosed by Jove
Spread havoc far and wide.

The author of the motto is not known, but one wonders if he was influenced by the line from Book I of Virgil's Aeneid.

Statio male fide carinis.

About the year 1660 Cork was a centre for the export of cattle to England but the Cattle Acts of 1663 and 1666 curtailed this trade and Cork turned to the provision trade with Holland, Spain, Portugal, and the British Colonies. Again this met with disapproval of English vested interests and the Navigation Acts of 1670 and 1671 severely limited this aspect of trade. It wasn't until the eighteenth century that a revival of this trade took place and in 1779 Cork, by reason of this trade, was considered the second city in Ireland. During the Napoleonic Wars the British Navy was supplied with Cork-cured beef. It is of interest that the provision trade was largely in the hands of Catholic merchants.

At the turn of the nineteenth century a serious crisis faced

98

the city in relation to the harbour. Over the years the river channels or canals as they were called had been silting up and about 1800 the depth of water in the main channel was only 4 feet at low water. It was all but impossible for ships to enter the city and only those of small tonnage could dock at the city quays. Even these were in danger at low water; they rested on the bottom and were in danger of keeling over. The quay walls were equally in very poor condition, consisting of only rubble masonry and built at low water level. The oncoming tides washed over the walls and the slob lands were inundated. Many of the larger vessels unloaded their cargoes at Passage where they were then transferred into barges and brought to the city – obviously, a very costly procedure.

All through the eighteenth century grants of money had been made by the Corporation and Government to help dredge the river but the money voted was insufficient and the technique of dredging was crude and too slow. In the middle of the century a scheme was proposed to dredge the river as far west as Macroom and a grant of £2,000 was sought but refused. By 1761 the Navigation or New Wall, running along what is now the Marina, had been built, as had the King's Quay at Blackrock. By 1800 the city quays as far east as the Customs House had been built.

In 1820 the Harbour Commissioners were formed and work on reclamation and dredging went on at a much faster pace. The 'Lee' dredger built locally was purchased, and it began dredging the channel. The silt was discharged into timber barges which were then towed ashore and discharged into the slob land behind the Navigation Wall, thus creating the City Park and the Marina. It was hoped to provide a channel giving a depth of eleven feet but the process was extremely slow, and in 1874 soundings showed a depth of only nine feet. Between 1867 and 1871 four steamhoppers were purchased, and the channel deepened to a depth of eleven feet by 1877. A 'Wingate' dredger was purchased in 1876 and by 1884 a channel depth of fourteen feet from Horse Head to Cork was achieved.

The construction of the quay walls, rubble masonry at

99

low water level, impeded the dredging of the quay sides and in 1855 sheet piling was commenced in order to permit a deepening of the channel to a depth from five to seven feet. In 1874 timber wharves were added to the south jetties. There were seven jetties, each 43½ feet long by 20 feet wide and they were separated by 120 feet of clear space. Within a short time the intervening spaces were filled in, and a total length of 1,130 feet was obtained.

The Cork Improvement and Cork Harbour Acts of 1875 authorized the Cork Corporation to replace two bridges over the river. One was a wooden foot bridge at the eastern end of Sundays Well and St Vincent's foot bridge was constructed. The second was Anglesea Bridge and this was replaced by the Parnell Bridge, a swivel giving a 50 foot clear passage, was constructed in 1882.

Work commenced on Penrose Quay in 1876 and in 1894 it was decided to extent it and to reconstruct Patrick's Quay. In 1903 legislation made possible the further improvements of the quays, and the Custom House and quay were acquired from the Board of Works. The City Railways Act of 1905 facilitated the construction of railway sidings on the quayside and by 1913 the Sherzer Rolling Lift bridges over the river had been completed.

About 1820 there were no light houses or buoys to mark the channel from Passage to Cork and work was started on this work. By 1859 the lighting and buoying from Horse Head to Cork was completed, there being twenty buoys from Cork to Passage and three from Passage to Cobh. The Blackrock, Dunkettle, and Horse Head Light Houses were constructed and by 1898 automatic lamps were installed in the Dunkettle and Lough Mahon Lighthouses.

The Custom House designed by William Hargrave, was completed by 1818 on land formerly a marsh. This was the site of a prison camp during the Napoleonic Wars and captured French soldiers were interned on this site. A tradition that parts of the quay walls were constructed by convict labour may have originated at this time.

In 1917 the Ford Organization purchased the land originally reclaimed from the slob land behind the Navigation

Wall but then the City Race Course. The Harbour Commissioners were anxious to acquire more property to provide for future expansion and purchased 153 acres of slobland at Tivoli from the Board of Works. Reclamation was begun and it now forms the Tivoli Industrial Estate.

CHAPTER 11

Henry Ford was born near the village of Ballinascarty, about 30 miles west of Cork City. In 1916 the Ford organization opened negotiations with the Cork Corporation for the purchase of land in the city with the intention of setting up a factory for the production of motor cars. The site chosen was that of the City racecourse, the location now known as the Marina. The site was extremely low lying, having been reclaimed from the river over a long number of years. As early as the middle of the eighteenth century a wall, called in turn, the New Wall and then the Navigation Wall, was constructed from the Municipal Buildings east along the river bank. Later during intensive dredging of the channel the silt had been pumped into the slob land behind the wall to facilitate reclamation. On completion of this work the area was designated City Park and later the City Race Course was built here.

One of the advantages of this site was its accessability to the quayside and sea-transport facilities. Negotiations reached a crucial stage in 1917 when agreement between the Corporation and the Harbour Commissioners and a Richard Woodhead of 91 Lord Street, Southport, England, acting as agent for Fords. At the same time agreement was reached with the Harbour Commissioners for the purchase of a strip of land on the bank of the river. An agreement dated 28 November 1917 granted the Ford Organization a lease of the property for 999 years at the annual fee of Id a year. It was an extensive tract of land circumscribed by the present Monaghan Road linking up with the Centre Park Road to the Marina and then back along the bank of the river to the site of the Ford factory.

The conditions of the agreement were:
(1) That Fords would pay a sum of £10,000 for the purchase of the land.

(2) Fords would take over the existing roadway and construct a new one at their expense.

(3) That 2,000 male adults would be employed at a minimum wage of a shilling an hour.

(4) That Fords would expend a total of not less than £200,000 on 'commercial shipping and manufacturing premises and out-offices or dwellings for industrial workers and in providing plant and equipment and in fitting out the same.'

(5) That Fords may pay £500 for the surrender of the Race Course Tenancy.

The agreement also provided for the acquisition of lands in the possession of Shandon Boat Club and the G.A.A., subject to the payment of £1,000 and compensation for the replacement of the pavilions. This option was never taken. The agreement was conditional on that all the conditions were to be implemented within a period of five years from the date of signing subject to 'strike, lock-outs, the Act of God, the King's enemies, riots and other inevitable and unforeseen events'. The Corporation, in turn would expedite the matters through Parliament. A similar agreement was signed with the Harbour Commissioners. The agreement – in addition to the financial arrangements – permitted Fords to enclose that portion of the river bank, mudland and foreshore and allowed them the right to dredge that portion of the river to obtain deep water.

The original agreement provided for the reconstruction of a roadway, the present Monaghan Road on the southern boundary of the property, but Fords requested that the location of this roadway be changed to the present Centre Park Road. The Corporation in an agreement dated 11 November 1921, acceded to the request with certain conditions. The road should be not less than 50 feet wide and should be completed within one year, of the signing of the agreement; if the cost of the Centre Park Road should be less then £15,000, Fords would remit the balance to the Corporation. On completion the road was taken over and maintained by the Corporation. It transpired that the road was not completed within the year but another agreement dated

17 July 1922 allows Fords a waiver on the conditions. Subsequently a third agreement dated 1 October granted permission to Fords to close all roads in the Marina for a day 'to prevent any prescriptive rights of way being acquired thereover'. In 1938 Fords had granted the Corporation permission to construct the link road between the Monaghan and Centre Park Roads.

The agreement of 17 July 1922 also set aside one of the most striking of the conditions of agreement. Fords were permitted to set aside that requiring them to employ a minimum work force of two thousand male employees. It had been apparent that this target could not be reached and the waiver only legalized the position. The establishment of Fords and in particular the minimum rate of one shilling an hour had created a minor sensation in the city. This rate was far in excess of the rates paid, not only in similar employments, but in many of the white collar jobs, and the opening of the factory saw the mass transfer of white collar workers to Fords. In addition to the assembly there was a foundry but this closed, appreciably reducing the work force. Many of these followed Fords to Dagenham England, and in the following years on their annual return home on holidays their boasting of their 'big' money earned for them the soubriquet 'The Dagenham Yanks'.

The coming of Fords tempted D.L. Kelleher to speculate on its effect on the city and he produced one of his inimatable ballads:

'Rumours of the Ford Motor Works rouse Padna to Reminiscence'

> When Padna all dust from grain loading
> Turned home like a knight in his mail
> From the Jetties, a kind of foreboding
> Was on him; he looked a bit pale.
>
> So deep were his thoughts and he walking
> Din Lucey he passed unawares;
> 'I declare to me God, you'd be talking,
> But, Padna, 'tis you're getting airs.'

Till Padna pulled up, 'Hello, Dinny,
Such news 'tis the devil an' all:
It'll near be the death of your Minnie
She's that gone about the New Wall.'

'Wat's that?' said Din Lucey, 'Disaster!'
Says Padna, 'And yet I don't know;
The Park'll be mills and it's faster
Than ever the money'll flow.'

'An' engines and steam and commotion
From Parnell's Bridge down to the Bank,
But, all though, I've a kind of a notion,
We'll still say the old times were grand.'

'The Buttera boys of a Sunday...
The piccolo tune was me dust
And well I remember the Monday
Berlins and Leander were best.'

'And Shandons and Lees and they training
For Queenstown and Glenbrook, and then
The regatta: they're off! Blues are gaining;
They're spurting! They're past it! Good Men!'

He looked at his palm: it was mighty
Could shift a half-hundred of grain:
A good share of years since the night he
First handled a cargo from Spain.

'I'm thinking' said he 'Dinny Lucey,
That bagging the grain is as clean,
And decent a trade as e'er you see
In all of the countries you've been.'

'I'll hate now to see my old Jetties
All soot and black smoke overhead.
A man growing old can't forget his
Fine boats of the days that are shed.'

Oh, my Padna, life's call is insistent,
And progress and smoke and great flame
Are the rules we obey; no resistant
Can alter the speed of the game.

Some time after the Russian Revolution of 1917 Fords opened negotiations with the Russian Government for the design and supply of a tractor with a view to a colossal sale. A prototype was produced but negotiations fell through and the machines were never produced.

The Ford plant is located on but a fraction of the land acquired in 1917. The remainder has been reclaimed and sites rented to many business in the city. Dunlops were one of the earliest to appreciate its advantages but in late years Gouldings Fertilizers, Oil companies, bakers and timber merchants have erected premises on the land. It is probable that the annual rental for these sites exceeds the total cost price of the property and in 1943 the Corporation sought advice as to the legality of the amended agreements. They were advised that the Corporation had no legal claims to the lands; that the agreement could only be revoked by Act of Parliament. The present value of the land is of course speculative but within the past few years Fords sold to the Harbour Commissioners, from whom they originally purchased the property, three acres at a cost of £15,000 per acre.

The construction of the Marina began in the middle of the eighteenth century to prevent the channel of the river 'from being choked with mud'. It extended from the Municipal Buildings, now the City Hall, east down the river. At about the same time the Kings Quay was built in Blackrock. Dredging operations were exceedingly slow due to the primative equipment available and in the case of the channel it was very costly. The mud had to be loaded into wooden barges which were towed ashore and then discharged into the slob land behind the Navigation Walk. Originally the Walk was only four feet wide with the river on one side and a wide expanse of mud and slob land on the other and was not then the popular and beautiful avenue as of later. Originally a right of way existed along the bank of the river and extended right into the city but this was set aside to facilitate the Ford Organization. In time a noble row of elm trees was planted along the Marina but these have been attacked by the Dutch Elm Disease and are now being cut down and will be replaced over the years. On the Navigation Walk near the site of the Ford works was the position of the old gun which every day was fired at mid-day to denote Greenwich mean-time. Alongside the Marina on the site of the old slob land is the Atlantic Pond once a swamp and infested with mosquitoes. To the south of the Marina near the Cleve Hill area is the 'Diamond Quarry'. There was a four days wonder in the city when 'diamonds and amethysts' were discovered. Investigation proved that the amethysts were quartz-coloured with black oxide of magnesium and the diamonds to be white quartz and rock crystals.

Blackrock village is an old fishing centre dating back for hundreds of years. In the sixteenth century the family of William Penn were in possession of Dundanion Castle and Penn stayed in the castle when he lived in Cork. Blackrock Castle stands on a site on which fortifications have stood since about 1582. In that year fortifications were erected to afford a safe anchorage and a protection against pirates and invasion. In 1601 James I granted a charter permitting 'a duty on fish to the Corporation for the support of Blackrock Castle'. In 1712 the Corporation permitted 'that the turf in the castle be sold by Samuel Woodroffe at 12d per kish to the Protestant inhabitants, not exceeding two kishes to each person'. The old castle was destroyed by fire and the Corporation decided to replace it with the present building which was completed in 1826 to the design of Thomas Payne. The cost was £1,000, £800 of which was contributed by the Corporation and £200 by the Harbour Authorities. By tradition the Mayors of Cork held Admiralty Court in the Castle and on 1 August it was usual for the members of the Corporation to 'have a public entertainment at the expanse of the city'. The ceremony of 'Throwing the Dart' began at the Mansion House in Henry Street and after the ceremony concluded with entertainment at Blackrock Castle. As early as 1614 the old castle was leased, and that year it was granted to William Terry and heirs provided that 'it were handed back to the Corporation upon any special cause of service', and it was also stated that Terry 'shall let the premises only to a freeman of Cork'. Later the building acted as a lighthouse and was later again rented out to a Cork family. Within the past few years it has been once again rented and on this occasion – as if reflecting on its ancient usage – has been converted into a restaurant.

Barry, James
Born Cork 11 Oct. 1741. Went to Dublin and exhibited *St Patrick baptizing the King of Cashel* in the Society of Arts at Shaws Court. The picture was bought for House of Commons, Dublin, but destroyed in fire. Barry was introduced to London in 1763 and later sent to Rome by Edmond Burke. Elected a member of Clementine Academy of Bologna. Reynolds and Barry offered to decorate St Pauls Cathedral gratuitously but the offer was refused. 1775 wrote *Enquiry to the Real & Imaginary Obstructions to the Acquisition of the Arts in England.* Decorated, gratuitously the walls of the Institution for the Encouragement of Arts. 1782: appointed Professor of Painting at the Royal Academy. 1799: expelled from Academy. 1806: died. Sir Robert Peel donated £200 for the funeral and his body was interred in St Pauls near Sir Joshua Reynolds.

Barter, Richard M.D.
Born Cooldaniel co. Cork 1802. Dispensary physician at Innascarra, Hon. Secretary of the County of Cork Agricultural Society. Studied and introduced to Ireland the practice of Hydropathy and opened the water-cure establishment at Blarney. It was through his efforts that Turkish Baths were introduced to Ireland and Great Britian. Died in Blarney 3 October 1870.

Bell, Robert
Born in Cork 1800 and educated at Trinity College. Wrote for newspapers and magazines and helped to revitalize the College Historical Society. Went to London and edited *Atlas.* Completed Sotheys' *Lives of the British Admirals.*
Other works: *Annotated Edition of the English Poets* in 24 volumes, *Life of Canning,* 1846, *Hearts and Altars,* 1852, *Ladder of Gold* 1856. Died London 12 April 1867.

Boyle, Richard, Earl of Cork

Born Canterbury 3 October 1566. Came to Ireland 23 June 1588, 'all my wealth was then £27'. Married a Limerick heiress 1595 who died a year later. Bought much property, accused of conspiracy but was cleared by Queen Elizabeth and crested clerk of the Munter Council. Purchased the 'Pilgrim' from Walter Raleigh. Brought the news of the Battle of Kinsale to Queen Elizabeth within 40 hours and suitably rewarded. Bought 12,000 acres of estate from Raleigh. Remarried 25 July 1603 and was knighted. Father of Robert Boyle, scientist who discovered 'Boyles Law' and kinsman of Elizabeth Boyle who married Spenser the poet in the Christ Church, South Main Street. Created Privy Councillor 1606, Lord Boyle, Baron of Youghal 1616, Viscount Dungarvan and Earl of Cork 1620, Lord Justice 1629 and Lord Treasurer 1631. 1641 fortified Lismore. Built, walled and fortified the town of Bandon at a cost of £14,000. 1649 commended by Cromwell for his activity. Died 15 September 1643 and buried in Youghal.

Barry, John Milner, Physician

Born Bandon 1768, educated Edinburgh, M.D. 1792 and returned to Cork. Founder of Cork Fever Hospital. Introduced vaccination into Ireland. Wrote medical treatises. Dies 1822.

Callanan, Jeremiah Joseph (sometimes James)

Born Cork 1795. Entered Maynooth but left in 1816 and entered Trinity. Assistant at school to William Maginn. Contributed to *Blackwood* and other magazines. Toured country collecting old ballads and legends, translating and rearranging them. Unfortunately many manuscripts lost. Other works: *Gougane Barra* 1826, *The Recluse of Inchidoney and other poems* 1830, *The Lay of Mizen Head* 1859, *Collected Poems* 1861.

Curran John Philpott. M.P., Lawyer and orator

Born Newmarket 24 July 1750. Educated at Midleton school and Trinity College where he was known as 'Stuttering Jack Curran'. Studied Divinity but on graduation went to London and entered the Middle Bar. Advocate of the cause of Catholic Emancipation and Rights and earned nickname of 'The Little

Jesuit of St Omer'. Married his cousin Miss Creagh in London. Won Major reputation at Cork Assizes in assault case against Lord Doneraile. Entered Parliament as M.P. for Kilbegaan in 1786 and remained in Parliament as M.P. for Rathcormack until 1797. Defended the United Irishmen including Wolfe Tone. No sympathy for Robert Emmett — annoyed at his daughter's secret engagement to Emmett. Appointed Master of the Rolls in 1806 but retired in 1814 on a Pension of £3,000 P.A. Attacked by paralysis and died 14 October 1817 in Brompton, England. Remains brought back and interred in Glasnevin. Bust in St Patrick's Cathedral.

Croker, Thomas Crofton
Born in Buckingham Square, Cork, 15 January 1798. Contributed to local journals. Went to London in 1818 but returned to Ireland in 1821 and began to collect stories and songs of the Southwest. 1824 *Researches in the South of Ireland.* 1825 *Fairly legends and traditions in the South of Ireland,* the second of which was illustrated by Maclise. Subsequently it was translated into German by the brothers Grimm. 1829 *Legends of the Lakes.* 1839 *Popular Songs of Ireland.* Croker also produced two humourous pieces *Barney Mahoney* and *My village versus your village.* Died 8 August 1854.

Connolly, Con., Trade-Unionist
Born Barrack Rd, (now Glengarriffe Rd.) Bantry, 23 June 1892. Eldest of 13 children, educated at Mercy Convent and National School, Bantry. Left school at 11 and came to Cork. Took up job as messenger boy with Lady's Well Brewery and worked from 7.30 a.m. to 7.30 p.m. Lived with aunt at Commons Road and attended night school at Buckley's school, Washington Street. Returned to Bantry in 1904. Worked in timber yard owned by Wm. Martin Murphy. Apprenticed to carpentry, without pay, until 1908. Worked on Garnish Island for £1 per week. Tried to organize tradesmen into union and sacked, and returned to Cork. Influenced by Big Jim Larkin. Joined 'Society of Carpenters and Joiners'. Elected to Union Committee 1915. Chairman of Union (Cork branch) 1922/3. Involved in six-months lock-out in 1923 and, as a result, with P.J. O'Brien, Jer.

Murphy (contractor) and John O'Connell (painter) helped form Joint Industrial Co. for Building Industry. Joint Chairman with Jer. Murphy for 17 years. Recommendations were always unanimous and invariably adopted. Chairman of National Federation of Building Trade Operators. Represented Ireland at Trade Union Conference at Margate in 1923. Participated in conference, re-amalgamation of British and Irish Unions, under chairmanship of Professor John Busteed. Elected to Cork Corporation in 1935 and active until 1967. Elected President of T.U.C. 1952/3. Early and vociferous advocate of Vocational Education.

Davis, Thomas Osbourne, Poet and Politician
Born Mallow 14 October 1814. Graduated from Trinity College and became a member of the bar 1835. Contributed articles to the *Dublin Morning Register.* Member of the Repeal Association. With Gavan Duffy and J.B. Dillon founded *The Nation* in which Davis published many of his ballad-poems. Died 16 September 1845. 1846 *The Poems of Thomas Davis.* Through *The Nation,* his ballads and his involvement with The Young Irelanders, Davis's influence on subsequent events was immense.

Emmet, Thomas Addis M.D., Barrister at Law
Brother of Robert Emmet, born in Cork (probably Henry Street) 24 April 1764. Educated at Mr Kerr's school, Trinity College, and Edinburgh. Travelled extensively in Germany, France and England. Read for two years at Temple and took Law degree, Michaelmas Term 1790 and admitted to Irish Bar. Married Jane Patten of Clonmel 1791. Joined Catholic Committee 1792. Defended Napper Tandy against the Viceroy (Earl of Westmoreland) with the Sheares Bros. and McNally (the informer) defended O'Driscoll on charge of seditious libel at Cork Assizes 1793. Defended United Irishmen in 1795 and himself took oath in Court. Active in United Irishmen in 1796 when military organization was formed. Member of the Directory 1797. Arrested in 1798 and imprisoned in Newgate and Kilmainham for one year. Interned at Fort George, Invernesshire and liberated in 1802 and went to Europe. In 1803 had interview with Napoleon, the 'worst enemy Ireland ever had'. Helped

organize United Irishmen into battalion to help French invasion of Ireland. Went to United States in 1804 and settled in New York where he defended the rights of escaped slaves to remain in New York. Refused to return to Ireland 'to walk over graves'. 'As to my children I hope they will love liberty too much ever to find a voluntary residence in an enslaved country'. Died 14 November 1827 and interred in St Mark's Church, Broadway New York.

England, John, Rev.
Born in Cork 23 September 1786. Entered Carlow College 1803 and founded schools for poor children of both sexes. Appointed to orders in Cork 1808 in the North Cathedral and Chaplain to the Prisons. Edited religious magazines and excelled in the cause of Catholic Emancipation. Once fined £500 in Court. Opposed hierarchy when they supported emancipation deal which would have deprived people of limited franchise. Parish Priest of Bandon in 1817. Bishop of Carolina and Georgia 1820. Published first Catholic magazine in America *Catholic Miscellany*. Wrote in favour of slavery. Travelled to Rome in 1832 and appointed Legate to Haiti. Died at Charlestown 11 April 1842. *Collected Works* published in five volumes.

Finn Barr
Born near Macroom in sixth century. Original name Lochan. Educated in either Munster or Leinster by McCorb. Travelled in Britain with Madioc. Founded monastery at Gougane Barra. Came in the valley of the Lee and settled and founded monastery at or near the present Gillabbey. It became a famous school and formed basis for the future city of Cork. Consecrated Bishop of Cork and died 623. Festival 25 September.

Forde, Samuel
Born Cork 5 April 1805. Fellow student of Daniel Maclise. Most of life spent in Cork. Works include *Vision of Tragedy* and *Crucifixion* which was painted in two days for Skibbereen Church. Died 29 July 1828.

Gallagher, Frank B.
Born Cork 1893. Joined Irish Volunteers; editor of *Irish Bulletin*. Imprisoned 1920. Editor of *Irish Press* 1931; Head of Government Information Bureau 1940. Publications: *Days of Fear* 1928, *The Four Glorious Years* 1953, *The Indivisable Island* 1957.

Gibbings, Robert
Born Cork 1889. Educated University College Cork and Slade School London. Noted artist and wood-carver; founder member of Society of Wood-Engravers. Taught Book Production in Reading University 1936. *Coconut Island* 1936, *Coming down the Wye* 1942, *Sweet Cork of Thee* 1951, *Lovely is the Lee, John Grahan, Convict* 1937.

Gregg John Rev. Bishop of Cork
Born Coppa 1798. Educated Trinity College, B.A. 1825: D.D. 1860. Appointed to Bethseda Chapel 1836; Trinity Church 1839 and remained there until 1862; Archdeacon of Kildare 1857; Bishop of Cork 1862. During his tenure of office the Cathedral of St Finnebarr was built, and he himself laid the foundation stone in 1865. It was opened on St Andrews Day 1870. Died 1878.

Hincks, Edward D.D., Philologist
Born in Cork 1792. Educated by father, a well-known orientalist, and later at Trinity where he became a scholar in 1810 and a fellow in 1813. Retired from the College in 1819 and from 1826 lived at Killileagh. Advocate of reform of the Established Church and of more extensive liberal system of education. Brilliant Oriental scholar and published a Hebrew grammar. An authority on Egyptian and Assyrian scholarship and was credited with the deciphering and interpretation of monuments in Babylon. Publications: *Transactions of the Royal Irish Academy*. 1854 *Report to the Trustees of the British Museum respecting certain Cylinder and Terra-cotta Tablets, with Cuneiform Inscriptions*, 1863 *A letter on the Polyphony of the Assyris-Babylonian Cuneiform Writing*. It was principally through his writing that it became possible for scholars to interpret the ancient writings. A bust of Edward Hincks is in the Cairo Museum. He was the brother of Francis Hincks who emigrated to Canada and is

credited with having played a major part in the setting up of the state of Canada. Died 3 December 1866.

Hogan, John, sculptor
Born in Tallow co. Waterford 1800, but family came to Cork soon after. Hogan was placed in a lawyers office. He soon showed artistic talent and sponsored by friends, the Royal Dublin Society and the Royal Irish Institution, he was sent to Rome in 1824. Studied at St Lukes' School in the Vatican and Capitol. Early works were *A Shepherd Boy, a pietà, Eve startled at the sight of David* and *A Drunken Fawn.* Returned home in 1829 and was awarded a gold medal by the Royal Dublin Society. His *Pietà* was purchased by the Carhelites for £400 and now it adorns the panel of the high altar in Clarendon Street. He returned to Rome and married. He was elected the first Irishman to the Society of the virtuosi of the Pantheon. At the outbreak of the Roman Revolution he returned to Ireland and settled in Dublin in 1848. Some of his work: Statues of Drummond and O'Connell, both in the City Hall, Dublin. A 'pietà' for St Francis church. Statue of Bishop Doyle for Carlow Cathedral. Died on 27 March 1858 and buried in Glasnevin.

Hogan Edmond, Rev. S.J.
Born Cork 1831. Studied in Rome D. Litt. Todd Professor of Irish Language, R.I.A. Publications: *Distinguished Irishmen of the Sixteenth Century,* Handbook of Irish Idioms, *The Irish People, The Irish Wolfhound, Onomasticon Gaedelicum* (still the definitive work on Irish placenames). Died in Dublin 1917.

Hennessy, Henry, Scientist
Born Cork 1826, civil engineer but studied physics and mathematics in his leisure hours and contributed to many journals. Invited to tale seat of physics at Catholic University by Newman in 1855. 1874 Professor of applied mathematics in R.C. of Science, 1858 F.R.S., 1870/3 Vice-President R.I.A. Retired 1891. Died in 1901 at Bray.

Horgan John J. Lt.D.
Born Janeville, Cork, 1881. Educated Clongowes Wood and Uni-

versity College Cork. Admitted a sollicitor in 1902 and Coroner for Cork County since 1914. LL.D. 1945. Prominent in public life. Contributed to the development of the Irish Local Government Managerial System. Chairman of the Cork Harbour Board and the Cork Incorporated Chamber of Commerce and Shipping. With John Boland M.P. carried through the registration of the Irish National Trade Mark and the Incorporation of the Irish Industrial Development Association. Writings mostly political and include: *Great Catholic Laymen* 1905, *Home Rule, a critical consideration* 1911, *The complete grammar of anarchy. By members of the War Cabinet and their friends* 1918, *The Cork City Management Act: Its origin, provisions, and Application.* 1929, *Parnell to Pearse: some recollections and reflections.* 1948, *The Policy of Eire, and Eire and the Communist challenge.* 1949, Articles in various journals and magazines. A play *The Nation Builders* was produced by the Cork Theatre Society 1905. Died 11 July 1967.

Jones, Henry Macnaughton, Surgeon
Born Cork 1845. Educated at Queens (now University College Cork) where at nineteen years of age he was a demonstrator in anatomy. M.D. and Professor of Midwifery. Founder of Eye, Maternity, and Victoria Hospitals. London in 1883. Published, *Diseases of Women,* Several volumes of verse, privately. Died 1918.

Mahony, Francis Silvester, Rev. (Fr. Prout)
Born in Cork c. 1805. Educated in France and Rome. Tutor at Clongowes Wood College (one of his pupils: Canon Sheehan). Retired from Orders and took up literature. Travelled extensively on the continent. Published *The Reliques of Father Prout* in Frasers Magazine and these were issued in separate form in 1836. Wrote *The Bells of Shandon* also for Frasers. A brilliant linguist. In *Moore's Plagarisms'* he traced their Greek and Latin origins. Wrote *The Goves of Blarney* in Italian at Lake Como, 25 May 1859 and translated it into French, Greek, and Latin. He travelled extensively in Hungary, Turkey, Greece and Egypt. 1846, he was Rome correspondent of the *Daily News* under Dickens. Articles subsequently published as *Facts and figures from Italy by Don Jeremy Savanorola, a Benedic-*

116

tine monk. 1858 to his death Paris correspondent of *The Globe*.
He returned to the Church. Died in Paris 18 May 1866. Buried
in St Anne's Shandon.

MacCurtain, Tomas, Freedom Fighter
Born Ballyknockane, co. Cork 1884. Educated at Burnfort National School and North Monastery Cork. First Republican
Lord Mayor of Cork. Murdered by British Forces at his home,
20 March 1920. Buried St Finnbarr's Cemetery, Cork.

O'Mahony, Eoin. B.L.,K.M. 'The Pope'.
Born Cork 1904. Educated locally and Clongowes Wood, University College Cork, Trinity College Dublin. Exhibitioner, aud-
itor and gold medallist U.C.C. Philosophical Society. Officer in
Cumann Gaeltacht, triple gold medallist in Historical Society
and double gold medallist in the Literary and Scientific Society,
Trinity College. Called to the Bar 1930 and to the English Bar
1933. State Counsel for Cork City and County. Committee of
the Munster Bar and Town Steward for Cork. Unsuccessful in
Dail Eelections and in seeking a nomination for the Presidency
in 1966. Member of Cork Corporation and Cork County Council. Genealogist and raconteur, broadcaster on Radio Eireann
'Meet the Clans'. Writings include *Catholic Organization in Holland* and *The Pathology of Democracy* as well as to various
journals. Died 15 February 1970.

Nagle Nano Foundress of Presentation Order
Born Ballygriffin co. Cork. 1728 Educated in Paris. 1763
Opened schools for the education of the poor in Dublin. 1771
Opened a house of the Ursulines in Cork. Disappointed that Ur-
sulines only taught the rich she opened her own schools. Died
South Presentation Convent 20 April 1784. 1791 Community
recognized by Pope. 1805 Community established as the Presen-
tation Order. Biography by Fr. J.C. Walsh.

O'Keefe Eoghan, Rev.
Born Glenville 1656. Married but on the death of his wife en-
tered the church and became P.P. of Doneraile. President of the
Bardic Meetings at Charleville. Some of his songs translated by
S.H.O'Grady.

O'Connor Frank (Michael O'Donovan)
Born Cork (over Wall's shop, Douglas Street) 1903, subsequently lived in Harringtons Square, Ballyvolane Rd.) Educated at St
Patricks N.S. where he came under the influence of Daniel
Corkery, North Monastery, but was rejected as being unsuitable
for secondary education and transferred to Technical School.
Active in War of Independence and acted as librarian to Cork
County and at Ballsbridge, Dublin. Achieved early success as
short-story writer and in the words of Yeats 'did for Ireland
what Chekhov did for Russia'. Has written novels, plays, and
two books of autobiography, and volumes of poetry. Active in
cause of the preservation of ancient monuments. Director of the
Abbey Theatre. Although very much influenced by Daniel
Corkery eventually broke with him and this is thought to have
been to O'Connor's disadvantage. Brilliant translator of old Irish
poetry and his reputation will probably rest on this more than
on the other media he has used. Lecturer at Harvard 1952 and
1954 and at Chicago University 1953. Doctorate 1966.

Mathew, Theobold, Rev. D.D.
Born Thomastown Co. Kilkenny, 10 October 1790. Educated at
home and entered Maynooth College September 1807. But left
in a short time and joined the Capuchin Order in Dublin. Ordained in 1814 and sent to Cork. Founded Literary Institutions
and industrial schools. 1838, with Rev. Nicholas Dunscombe,
Richard Dowden and William Martin he signed Temperance
Pledge at public meeting and so formed Temperance Society.
His two brothers were brewers. The movement extended to England and Scotland and 600,000 members enrolled in 1847. Nom-
inated 'dignissimus' for See of Cork but not appointed. 1848 Attacked by paralysis but recovered. 1849 Mission to America and
honoured by formal reception by Senate and entertained by
President. Retired to Cobh and died 8 December 1856.

Murphy Seamus R.H.A.
Born Mallow 1907 (Fair Lane). Came to Cork 1909 and edu-
cated at St Patricks N.S. where he came under the influence of
Daniel Corkery. Attended School of Art, Cork and won Gibson
Scholarship and studied in Paris 1932/3. Now lives at Wellesley

118

Tce. and has studio at Watercourse Rd. Elected to R.H.A. 1943. Published *Stone Mad* 1950. Designed Blackpool Church under patronage of Mr Wm. Dwyer. Hon. L.L.D. National University 1969.

Maclise Daniel R.A.
Born Cork 25 January 1811. Studied at Cork Academy (Sharman Crawford School of Art). First commission to illustrate Croftons Crokers *Fairly Legends*. Executed portrait of Sir Walter Scott. Opened studios in Cork. 1827 Went to London and studied at the Royal Academy. 1830 Paintings exhibited at the Royal Academy. 1937 Elected an Associate. 1840 Elected a Royal Academician. Executed frescoes for Houses of Parliament. Illustrated first edition of Moore's *Melodies*. Died 25 April 1870.

Maginn William LL.D. Author
Born in Cork July 1793 or 1794. Educated Cork and Trinity College where he attained the degree of LL.D. at 23 years of age. Contributors to *Blackwood's* magazine from 1817. Married in 1823. Opened school in Cork but went to London. 1824 went to Paris as correspondent of the Representative. 1830 Co-founder of *Fraser's Magazine*. 1838 Published the first of his *Homeric Ballads*. 1927 *Whitehall of the day of George IV*. 1844 *John Manesty*.

Maguire, John Francis, Politician and Writer
Born in Cork c. 1815. Called to the Irish Bar in 1843. M.P. for Dungarvan 1852 and from 1865 to 1872 as M.P. for Cork. Supporter of the Liberal Party and agitated for the disestablishment of the Church, land reform and female suffrage. 1870 Joined the Home Rule Party. Articles on Home Rule, first published in the *Cork Examiner* were subsequently published in book form 1871. 1857 *Rome and Its Rulers*. 1862 *Life of Fr Mathew*. 1868 *Irish in America*. 1871 *The next Generation*. Created a Knight Commander of Saint Gregory. Died near Cork 1 November 1872.

Mac Swiney, Terence

Born Cork 1883. B.A. Royal University, taught himself Irish. Founded school. Founded magazine *Fianna Fail*. Wrote plays. *The Revolutionist* was performed at the Abbey 1921. Interned 1916, M.P., for MidCork 1918 and elected Republican Lord Mayor of Cork. Arrested and imprisoned in Brixton Prison. Went on hunger strike which lasted until his death after seventy-four days in 1920. Publications: *Battle Cries* 1918, *Despite Fools Laughter* 1918, *Principles of Freedom,* published posthumously.

MacLiammoir Michael, actor, author, artist

Born Cork 1899. Educated Cork and Spain. Appeared on stage in London 1911. Returned to Ireland and helped found The Gaelic Theatre in Galway and the Gate Theatre Dublin 1928. Has played all major roles in the theatre and toured all over the world. Achieved most outstanding success recently in 'one-man shows'. *The Importance of being Oscar* and *I must be Talking to my Friends.* Deeply respected for his decision to remain in Ireland instead of taking his talents to more lucrative markets. Brilliant linguist. He has written in both Irish and English, plays, novels, short stories and autobiography. He has produced and designed stage sets. He is a consummate artist. Some publications: *All for Hecuba* 1946. *Put Money in thy Purse* 1952. *I'll met by Moonlight* 1957. *Each Actor on his Ass* 1960. *Aisteoir idir dha Crich* 1960. *Theatre in Ireland* 1964. *An Oscar of no Importance* 1968.

O'Faolain Sean

Born Half Moon Street Cork 1900 (he lived in three separate houses, over Mathew's, over Arthur's electrical shop and in one other). Educated at St Josephs, Mardyke and University College Cork where he took an M.A. and later at Harvard. Like O'Connor, influenced by Daniel Corkery. He has excelled in various forms, novels, short stories, autobiography, plays, and historical biography. Active in War of Independence and took the Republican side in Civil War. Lecturer in American Universities. Brings a great deal of scholarship to bear on his writing. Shares with O'Connor the pinnacle of Irish writing. Lives near Dublin.

O'Riordain Sean P.
Born Cork 1905 National Teacher and studied in Europe. Professor of Archaeology University College Dublin. Editor of *Journal of Cork Historical and Archaeological Society*. 1937 to 1943. Excavated Hill of Tara. Publications: *Antiquities of the Irish Countryside* 1942; *Tara; the monuments on the Hill* (pamphlet) 1954, *New Grange and the Bend on the Boyne* 1964 (in collaboration with Glyn Daniels).

Sharman-Crawford, Arthur Frederick, Philantropist
Born Dublin 1862. Educated at Eastbourne College. Justice of the Peace for County Cork. Chairman of the Cork Technical Instruction Committee. Governor of the Cork Dairy Institute. Manager of Beamish and Crawford, brewers. Undertook cost of building addition of Sharman Crawford Municipal School of Art, Cork, and the Sharman Crawford Technical School, Cork. Donated £20,000 to defray the cost of the West or main Portal St Finnbarre's Cathedral, Cork.

Pain, George, Architect
Born London 1799. Came to Cork 1818 to design County Gaol and settled here. Excellent water colour artist. Contributed a great deal to the architectural life of the city. Designs: County Gaol 1818; Holy Trinity 1825, The Citys County Club 1826; The Court House 1835: Blackrock Castle; The Independent Chapel; St Patricks Church 1836, Charlotte Quay; O'Callaghans Gate, Lr. Road; and the interior of St Mary's Cathedral & Christ Curch. Died 1838.

Sheares the Brothers, Henry and John
Sons of Henry Sheares, Banker. Both born in Cork, Henry 1753. John 1766. Educated at Trinity. Henry joined the army but renounced it and called to the Bar 1789. John called to the Bar 1788. Both went to Paris in 1792 and made the acquaintance of French revolutionary leaders Roland, Brissot etc. Present at execution of Louis XVI. Returned to Ireland on same boat as Daniel O'Connell. The brothers joined the United Irishmen, John chairing several public meetings. After attending the funeral of Rev. William Jackson in 1798 warrants were issued

for their arrest. After the seizure of most leaders of the U.I. in Bandon in 1798, John became Chief Organizer. Brothers betrayed by Captain Armstrong and arrested 21 May. They were defended by Curran, Plunkett, and McNally (the traitor), and after an enforced all-night sitting both were convicted, although there was serious doubt as to Henry's involvement. Executed in front of Newgate 14 July 1798.

Thompson, William

Born Roscarberry 1785. Benevolent Landlord. One of the first to conceive and put into practice the idea of co-operatives and he established one at Carhoogarriffe, Skibbereen. One of the original thinkers in the theory of socialism and quoted by Marx. Works: *An Inquiry in the Principles of the Distribution of Wealth most conducive to Human Happiness* 1824. *Appeal of one half of the Human Race, Women, against the Pretentions of the Other half, Men, to retain them in Political and thence, in Civil and Domestic Slavery* 1825. *Labour Rewarded; The Claims of Labour and Capital Conciliated, or how to secure to Labour the whole Products of its Exteriors. By one of the Idle Classes* 1827. *Practical Directions for the Establishment of Communities on the Principles of Mutual Co-operation* 1830.

Voynich, Ethel Lilian, Authoress

Born Cork 1867, youngest daughter of Prof. George Boole, author of *The Laws of Thought*. Married Polish Count. 1897. *The Gadfly* a novel published in 1897 with its hero a revolutionary patriot and set in Italy caused a sensation and was an immediate success, selling two and a half million copies in England and America alone; bestseller also in Russia and China. Other works: *An interrupted Friendship; Olive Latham; Frank Raymond; Put off thy Shoes.* Died 1947.

Walsh, Edward

Born Derry 1805, son of Cork Militia man. Taught school in Millstreet and at Toureen in 1837. Contributed to the *Nation*. Appointed schoolmaster to the convict station on Spike Island but dismissed for his friendship with John Mitchell. Appointed schoolmaster to the Cork Workhouse and served there to his death. Editor of *The Jacobite Relics of Ireland*. Collector and expert in the fairy lore of Ireland and published two volumes of poetical translations from the Irish complete with the original text. *Irish Popular Songs* 1847. Hayes in his *Ballads of Ireland* says of him ...his translations preserve all the peculiarities of the old tongue, which he knew and spoke with graceful fluency. His ballads are the most literal and characteristic that we possess.' Died in Cork 1850.

Windele, John, Antiquarian
Born Cork 1801. Renowned antiquarian, travelled the countryside collecting material and folklore. Preserved many Ogham inscriptions. Collected Ancient Irish Manuscripts which were bought by the R.I.A. in 1865; 170 volumes, 42 entirely in Irish. 1839 Published in Cork *Historical and Descriptive Notices of the City of Cork and its vicinity, Gougane Barra, Glengarriffe and Killarney*. Contributed to many other journals. Died at Blairs Hill, Cork, 28 August 1865.

MORE MERCIER BOOKS

THERE IS A BRIDGE AT BANDON

Kathleen Keyes McDonnell

Bandon — 'Droichead na Banndan': Bridge of Bandon — has
a unique history. This pleasant market town, the creation of
Richard Boyle, first Earl of Cork, was once the enclave of
an aggressive Protestantism — 'Turk, Jew, or Atheist may
enter here, but not a Papist.' It was geographically and
ethnically inevitable that when the struggle for Irish independence began in 1916 Bandon should at once become a focal
point in the conflict. The planter tradition was still strong
here, deeply rooted in the rich soil of the valley of the Bandon but at the same time a new spirit, that of Pearse and
Plunkett, was abroad and this was soon to sweep away
British rule in the South of Ireland. One man more than any
other typified this spirit in West Cork: William Keyes
McDonnell of Castlelack, near Bandon. In this book his
widow, Kathleen Keyes McDonnell, paints a picture of her
husband, the eternal type of the revolutionary patriot, the
rebel who also cares deeply for tradition. In doing so, she
adds a significant footnote to the history of the War of Independence. The Bandon area saw intense guerilla activity.
Tom Barry operated in the vicinity of Bandon; and both
the R.I.C. and the British Army were based in Bandon, including units of the Essex Regiment who were to become
notorious for their harshness and repression. Mrs McDonnell
leaves nothing out; we feel the tension of a community
divided against itself, the hatred and suspicion engendered
by the presence of an alien Army of Occupation. Indeed
here, in little is the North of Ireland today.

This is a work of history that the events of the last few
years has made fiercely topical.

(HARD COVER)   Approx Price £2.85

MUNSTER AT WAR

Barry O'Brien

For more than two thousand years wars have been waged in Ireland – indeed it could have often been described, like Flanders, as the cockpit of Europe. The author starts with the Viking invasion and Brian Boru, and goes on to deal with the long struggle that has existed between the Irish and English in Munster during the sixteenth and seventeenth centuries. The book clearly relates this conflict to the much wider struggle that was taking place for the domination of Europe.

This book considers in fascinating detail such events as the Massacre at Smerwick and the two sieges of Kinsale and the exploits of such men as Patrick Sarsfield, William of Orange, and John Churchill and various conflicts, civil and foreign, at the end of the eighteenth century. *Munster at War* is a vivid and colourful book, the fruit of many years research, at once scholarly and exciting.

(HARD COVER)   Approx Price £3

THE BEST OF TONE

Edited by Proinsais MacAonghusa and Liam Ó Reágáin

Theobard Wolfe Tone (1763–1798) has been the greatest single influence on Irish political life. This great humanist of Protestant birth was the most enlightened Irishman of his day and the story of his short life in Ireland, the United States and France is an amazing tale of incredible courage, high intelligence, patriotism and adventure. The best of Irish political thinking has been based on his writings and philosophy but for a considerable time these writings have not been readily available. Few Irishmen have had the opportunity of reading Tone for themselves. Now Proinsias MacAonghusa and Liam Ó Reágáin, editors of the *Best of Connolly* and *The Best of Pearse* present his most significant writings in a book destined to play as direct a role in the making of the new radical Ireland as their two other collections already have done.

Of Tone's 1791 Freedom Manifesto James Connolly wrote: 'It would be hard to find in modern Socialist literature anything more broadly International in its scope and aims, more definitely of a class character in its methods, or more avowedly democratic in its nature than this manifesto, yet, although it reveals the inspiration and methods of a revolutionist acknowledged to be the most successful organizer of revolt in Ireland since Rory O' More, all his present day professed followers constantly trample upon and repudiate every one of these principles and reject them as a possible guide to their political activity. The Irish Socialist alone is in line with the thought of this revolutionary apostle of the United Irishmen'.

Price 70p

A NATURAL HISTORY OF IRELAND

Christopher Moriarty

This is the first Natural History of Ireland for the beginner –
school pupil or adult – who wants a brief outline of the subject.

Concentrating on the common plants and animals, the
book is divided into two parts, the first half deals with the
country as a whole, the second is a county by county guide
showing where the animals and plants can be found. English
rather than scientific names have been used, and technical
terms kept to a minimum.

Price £1.25

DICTIONARY OF IRISH WRITERS
Volume 111 (Literature in Irish)

Compiled by Brian Cleeve

This third volume in the Dictionary of Irish Writers series
records every major writer in Irish and Latin from earliest
times together with details of their work. The list of anonymous literature and the major scribal compilations such
as the Books of Leinster and Ballymote are also recorded.

For the student or interested reader this book will prove
an invaluable guide to the wealth of Irish literature.

Price £1.00

If you would be interested to receive
announcements of forthcoming publications
please send your name and address to:
THE MERCIER PRESS
4, Bridge Street,
Cork, Ireland

First published in the Netherlands
Made and printed by Van Boekhoven-Bosch NV
Utrecht, Holland.